YOUR CITY IS WAITING ON YOU

Becky Haas

Cover design by Tanner Clements, Johnson City, Tennessee

Author's photo by Eddie Lambert Photography, Kingsport, Tennessee

Connect with the author: Bhaascityreach@gmail.com

Follow "Your City is Waiting on You" on Facebook https://www.facebook.com/yourcityiswaitingonyou/

ISBN: 1973812886
ISBN 13: 9781973812883

ENDORSEMENTS

Jesus did not just give us a Great Commission; He offered us a Great Partnership. Becky Haas entered into that partnership and her journey to being an ordinary person doing extraordinary deeds is riveting. Fasten your seat belt! The same offer is available for you!

Dave Thompson
Senior Vice President, Harvest Evangelism, Transform Our World Network

It is not often that one gets the opportunity to provide insight into another person's life, especially a minister of the Gospel. In this case it is about one who though working in the secular world continues to use the anointing of the Spirit to advance the Kingdom of God in the local community. Becky Haas had second thoughts about working with the Johnson City Police Department as the organizer and facilitator of a community crime reduction program, but as the next three years proved, she was the right person for the job. The success of the program and the vision that she obtained through reliance on God's power, wisdom and goodness became a story of how to unite people and create places of empowerment. As a result, diverse groups of people began working together to change their community through active partnerships and investment of personal time. Road blocks and obstacles were cleared in project after project. Becky continued to build her own skills through much education and never considering "No" as an answer to achieving possibilities. Becky Haas is a leader, who has a compassionate heart, great faith in God and a desire to create answers that work. She has inspired many in our community on a personal level and has the acclaim of other leaders on a state and national level. Read this book and you will understand what I mean. Read this book and discover ways you can help make your community a better place to live.

Randall E. Jessee PhD,
Senior Vice President, Frontier Health

Heartfelt thanks to my dear friend, Dorsey Reed, for your many years of encouragement and mentoring. You taught me the importance of setting spiritual goals in order to experience an increase in Kingdom influence, to which this book testifies of. Thank you to Jan Boyd for your help editing, and the grace with which you reminded me to shorten my sentences. Thank you also for affirming this book had a message to be shared as encouragement for others. Thank you to Ann Eargle for your editing skills and for sharing your experience with me about publishing a book. Thank you hardly seems adequate to Dr. Andi Clements. You not only helped to edit the manuscript but you walked through much of this story with me. I'm grateful for your friendship and how you never doubted that God wanted to do big things in our city. Lastly thank you to my precious husband Jonathan for your constant love and support, and for believing this story should be told long before I did.

TABLE OF CONTENTS

INTRODUCTION

In December of 2012 I was hired by the local police department as the Director of an eight hundred thousand dollar grant-funded crime reduction project while the grant was still in the planning stages and the department preparing submission of a funding proposal. This project was going to be aimed at reducing drug related and violent crime in the two neighborhoods in our city where historically these types of crimes were highest. When I came on board the project was in the middle of a six-month planning period. There were three months remaining to lay out the final blueprint of outcomes we hoped to accomplish and then finish writing the application. The grant required bringing together state and local service agencies and various non-profits who would collaborate on identifying the causal crime factors in these neighborhoods, and determine what measures would eliminate these factors and implement evidence-based programming to actually reduce the crime. Our programs had to address four areas: prevention; law enforcement; neighborhood revitalization; and offender reentry.

Before this time my career consisted of no criminal justice experience or any work in city government. Among many objectives, this crime reduction grant had as an outcome to "reduce recidivism." The first time I heard the word "recidivism" I had to look it up in the dictionary and that's where I learned that it was a word used to describe someone previously incarcerated who returned to criminal behavior. Not only was recidivism a foreign concept to me, but now I had to help reduce it! My prior years of work experience included twenty four years working at my home church serving in various capacities of ministry and administration as well as eight years of employment at a state university. At the university I developed and executed training programs on subject matters ranging from Human Subject Safety compliance in medical research to Child Passenger Safety education. I was also a passionate volunteer in the community serving on the Board of Directors of an eight-county Head Start program, serving on a Prenatal Coalition for the local Health Department, and facilitating character education classes for parents and teenagers involved in the Juvenile Justice System in two counties. My criminal justice experience may have been lacking when I joined the police department, but my foundation of truth found in God's Word more than compensated for my lack of secular training in this field. It is some of these truths that I'm sharing in this book. I believed in my heart then, as I do now, that God had plans for my life to make a difference and if reducing crime was now His plan for me, then that's exactly what would happen. I trusted God would be with me at work, that His favor was there to assist me, and I knew He had promised to bless everything I put my hand to. I accepted for every question I would face, He would have an answer, and for every problem He would have a solution.

Throughout all the years I have walked with God, I have experienced His faithfulness in many ways, but it was when I stepped into this servant role that I knew what was happening were "God-sized" interventions. I recognized too that I was provided an opportunity to learn firsthand about needs and services within my community, and there I saw how many open doors exist for serving others. That is the focus of this book. To make a miraculous story short, by God's favor I brought together a wonderful group of agency partners who ultimately created nineteen programs we implemented in two neighborhoods and reduced crime over a period of three years. In August of 2014, just halfway through our grant cycle, the program received national recognition by winning a prestigious criminal justice award. I accepted the award on behalf of my community partners at a national criminal justice conference surrounded by members of the President's cabinet along with senior staff and advisors from governors' offices from many of the fifty states. Our program went on to be listed by the U.S. Department of Justice as a "Success Story." At the conclusion of the grant in March of 2016, thirty-five agencies had joined with law enforcement to fully implement all nineteen crime reduction efforts. Through this grant, with the help of community partners, I was able to implement programs that included mentoring by police officers for at-risk youth living in public housing; initiate and facilitate a monthly neighborhood watch group and organize a safety program for the Downtown merchants; start a community garden; co-author a city ordinance which created a process where residents living in high-crime neighborhoods could apply for additional street lighting which resulted in fourteen new street lights installed in one neighborhood; see a 40% reductions in 911 calls in the residential high-crime area; initiate proactive policing details which resulted in 64 arrests Downtown over one six-month period; and create the first probation program of its kind in the state to reduce recidivism among high risk, felony offenders with addictions. At the end of the grant, the probation program was transferred to the state department of corrections, which now operates and fully funds the program as their own and is replicating it across the state. Due to the high level of community participation in this program, the cost to the state was only twelve dollars a day for an offender to attend; instead of seventy four dollars a day to be incarcerated as was typical. The criminal court judges who were part of the development team for this program now consider it a vital resource to the court that allows them to avoid sending some individuals back to prison for new crimes or probation violations. While in this probation program the individuals receive services such as counseling, drug and alcohol treatment, life skill courses, job readiness evaluation and job skills training which equip them to overcome the barriers they face to successfully break the cycle of crime in their lives.

Throughout the life of the grant, collectively the partnering agencies had provided in-kind services worth over seven hundred thousand dollars to the city, in addition to the grant monies we had received. With this as my track record, City Commissioners approved a new Coordinator position at the police department to oversee programming to prevent crime, for which they retained me. Never in my wildest dreams while attending Rhema Bible Training Center, or during the many years I spent on staff at my home church, would I have thought that God's paths for me would include reducing crime through police programs. Our department has now hosted the Chief of Police and a team from the Mayor's office from a larger city in our state inquiring about our program as well as a delegation from a neighboring state who considered applying for a similar crime reduction grant. Again in November of 2016, our program received national recognition from an international foundation seeking to support local initiatives that enhance public safety in innovative ways through civic engagement. This recognition brought with it a fifteen-thousand dollar award to our department. Looking back on all this I truly stand amazed and give glory to God for the things HE has done!

In every police department, any citizen over the age of 21 can submit a request to ride along with an officer during his or her shift to see police work through the eyes of police. I've done several ride alongs and was amazed each time at the bravery of our officers responding to calls that would instinctively have sent me heading in the other direction instead of into the crisis being described by dispatchers. Working at the police department I have been able to catch a glimpse of our community that I'd never seen before. I've felt like I was on a ride-along with God. In much the same way, through my daily work I have been able to witness firsthand the vast number of hurting and broken people that God sees every day. I am in a position to hear their stories, meet many of them face to face and observe their challenges caused by abuse, neglect, violence, poverty, addictions or a lifestyle of crime. Seeing these things, I began praying and wondering how God could rescue these who were hurting. How could He use me to help the hurting in our city? By working closely with local agencies, and state and federal organizations to implement crime reduction programs, I began to see all the open doors that existed in our town where churches could become involved. Churches are always encouraging members to "bring a guest to church," which is important but what if the church members went to where these people lived and worked instead? What if church members volunteered two hours a week to help tutor kids with their homework; or started a kickball league for children who have little or no contact with their dads; or collected food and clothing to donate to kids attending public schools who are listed as "homeless," or took a half-day training session to become a host family that could provide short-term, emergent care for young children whose parents were experiencing a crisis? It seemed to me if church leaders and congregations could see what I was seeing, no church would ever need to create a community outreach program again or be left to wonder of its effectiveness. Serving – it almost seems too easy.

Every town in America has a similar infrastructure as my town. They all have the same systems. Public housing, public schools, corrections and reentry, services for the elderly, at-risk youth programs, and the list goes on and on. By following the model for taking ministry out into the marketplace just as Jesus demonstrated for us in the four gospels, you will find your town is literally "WAITING ON YOU" to come. There are doors standing open for you to love the unlovely, care for the broken, and reach thousands of unchurched in your community. By choosing to serve others, which is the ministry Jesus said is the greatest ministry; you can build genuine relationships with individuals in your city that you likely would have not met in any other way. By forming these caring relationships can lead to opportunities to pray for them and share the gospel with them. In traditional evangelism programs we've been taught to address the unchurched first about spiritual matters when actually they don't even understand their greatest need is a spiritual one. If FIRST we meet a physical need like a winter coat, food for the pantry, removing fallen trees from the yards of a shut-in or a couple of nights a week helping adults earn their high school equivalency so they can get a better job, we will walk through wide open doors and find hearts are standing open because we have shown them that we care. Have you ever considered preaching the gospel but doing it without speaking in "Christian-ese?" Love and kindness are a universal language that is spoken by all.

I've discovered a multitude of ways people can become involved within the systems and agencies in their town that most churches may have never before considered. For instance, I witnessed how something as easy as starting a community garden could cultivate a safe activity for the children of a neighborhood and also helped to provide a healthy food source for them and their families. In corrections, I have seen those returning to the community from incarceration face tremendous barriers to breaking the cycle of crime, but those barriers are a place for the church to show love and kindness. I never knew until I became involved working with the reentry community that every year hundreds of thousands of people are released from state and federal prisons only to return again within a few months or years. Helping these returning citizens successfully acclimate to the community requires networking to find housing, employment, and transportation and most likely there will be a need to build a whole new set of friends because their old ones were fellow drug addicts or they had engaged in criminal activities together.

In spring of 2014, the Lord laid on my heart to begin assembling faith-based leaders at the police department on a bi-monthly basis to share with them of all these opportunities. It seemed to me God was laying out a blueprint on how to pastor a city. I would have the directors or agency staff share needs or service opportunities these churches could fill. Some were small needs like providing money for bus passes to be given to the agencies working with the homeless or those previously incarcerated so individuals can take the bus to the health clinic or to a job interview. Leaders learned how they could encourage their church members to volunteer as host homes for young children needing short-term emergent care in a time of family crisis in order to avoid young children being left alone or going into the state foster care system. They learned of the needs of grandparents who are now raising their grandchildren while the parents are incarcerated or absent because of drug addiction.

In Luke 10: 1-2 we read, "Now after this the Lord chose and appointed seventy others and sent them out ahead of Him, two by two, into every town and place where He Himself was about to come (visit). And He said to them, The harvest indeed is abundant [there is much ripe grain], but the farmhands are few. Pray therefore the Lord of the harvest to send out laborers into His harvest." Jesus told us two things about the harvest. He said it is abundant and it is ripe. When the crop is ripe it means it's time for it to be gathered in. Those who have never submitted to Jesus Christ as their Lord and Savior are the crop He's speaking of. God is described as the patient farmer in James 5:7 who is waiting expectantly for the precious harvest. "So be patient, brethren, as you wait till the coming of the Lord. See how the farmer waits expectantly for the precious harvest from the land. See how he keeps up his patient vigil over it until it receives the early and late rains." What could be a more precious harvest from this land than the people who live on it? God has harvest on His mind. The greatest Farmer is waiting on the largest harvest of all time. Your city it is full of people who are waiting to see the love of God demonstrated to them and then to hear the gospel of His goodness. They are ripe for this and they are precious to God. Are you ready to meet them?

The first several of the chapters of this book contain truths from God's Word that I trusted in as I went out into the marketplace of our city. The Lord's directive to me for writing was to do so in such a way that anyone could, in some way, replicate my story. It might not be from a position working in a police department, but these truths will work wherever God has planted you. As you read these truths, realize they are tools God is giving you to influence the lives of many within your city. There is no one who loves your city more than He does but you may be the way He has planned to reach them. So these foundational chapters are to help you recognize how He is there to help you as you go, and it is more than enough to get the job done. I know there are some who are already experiencing God-sized favors and bringing solutions to community challenges so to you I hope these words accelerate your impact even more. 2 Peter 1:4 from the Message Bible says, "Everything that goes into a life of pleasing God has been miraculously given to us by getting to know personally and intimately, the One who invited us to God. The best invitation we ever received! We were also given absolutely terrific promises to pass on to you – your tickets to participation in the life of God after you turned your back on a world corrupted by lust." His promises are your tickets to participate! Fill your heart and mind with His promises as you go out into your city in your daily activities. Fully expect that His promises will allow you to receive His favor and empowerment enabling you to be a blessing far beyond what your natural abilities alone could accomplish. Dream big and raise your expectations for God to provide solutions for the problems facing your community through you. As you do, you will be building relationships with people you find who are hurting and don't know of God's great love for them. The harvest is ripe and He is waiting expectantly on His precious fruit. Stop asking for God to open doors to access the fields of harvest in your city but instead step through the ones already standing open as outlined in these pages. You might be surprised to find that your city is out there waiting on you.

JESUS CAME TO SEEK AND TO SAVE

*"For the Son of Man came to seek and
to save that which was lost."*

Jesus (Luke 19:10)

Every day we wake up in the middle of a true story that has been going on a long time. This story is about God and His love for His family. This God story has a beginning, middle and somewhere along the way before it ends, it includes the time we are living in today. The story is progressive and nothing our society experiences ever catches God by surprise. When you read the Bible beginning with the account of creation in Genesis, you see that God has always had a plan for man. Better yet, God has consistently communicated that plan to man. There is comfort in knowing that God communicates to us in the Bible how to live during every period of this ever-advancing story, even telling us what we can expect.

In Isaiah 60:1-3 we read, "Arise [from the depression and prostration in which circumstances have kept you—rise to a new life]! Shine (be radiant with the glory of the Lord), for your light has come, and the glory of the Lord has risen upon you! For behold, darkness shall cover the earth, and dense darkness [all] peoples, but the Lord shall arise upon you [O Jerusalem], and His glory shall be seen on you.

And nations shall come to your light, and kings to the brightness of your rising." Many times God's dealings with Jerusalem in the Old Testament can be viewed as a type of His dealings with Zion or the Church. This prophetic word for Jerusalem certainly can also point to the day we are living in.

Understand that God has picked you to live in this generation. Isaiah prophesied that it is a generation that is capable of seeing two views at the same time. First is the view of dense darkness. In my lifetime I've never seen a time that seems as dark as the times in which we live. All of our institutions that were once thought to be unshakeable are now being shaken and many of them crumbling. Governments, financial institutions, healthcare and educational systems have all undergone great change in the past several decades. Cities are experiencing all-time highs of crime rates, corruption, violence, broken families and an epidemic of addiction, which make up the news daily. This is the view of dense darkness. But Isaiah told us there is another view on which we must set our eyes. That is the view of the glory of God radiating and the brightness of His light resting upon us in such a way that nations and kings will be drawn to this brightness. Light is the brightest where darkness is the densest. We are living in a day where there is an opportunity for the Church to shine its brightest since it began on the Day of Pentecost. As we witness the worst of the worst in the world we can have great expectations to experience the best of the best in the kingdom of God. The Church began in the Book of Acts by being filled with the power of the Holy Spirit. How much more does our generation need to see the power of God demonstrated within the Church today?

Consider the Parable of the Great Feast as recorded in Matthew 22:1-14. First the king sent his servants to invite people to the wedding feast from all over town. They began to offer excuses for why they could not come. Then the king told his servants to go into the street corners and invite everyone they saw. I'm going to take some liberties here and propose to you that it's my conviction that the first groups invited were those involved in religious activities and attending churches filled with the traditions of men. Since the late 1960's, we have seen the Holy Spirit moving among every denomination causing an immense stirring that brought many people to the fullness of the baptism of the Holy Spirit. This move was followed by decades of in-depth Bible Study by not just a few but by the masses. Bible teachers were raised up around the world. When I was a child growing up in church I was not aware of anyone that was a Bible teacher. I only knew of pastors and missionaries who were what we considered full-time ministers. During this sovereign move of God, we have seen a new breed of church born. Civic auditoriums filled with worshippers were not commonplace in the 1950's or 60's. Now through ministries like Hillsongs, Jesus Culture, Elevation, and Passion the masses travel to join tens of thousands nightly in worship to our King. It is now common to find hundreds or thousands gathered for heartfelt worship in church buildings, school gymnasiums or renovated shopping centers, listening to anointed teaching from the Word of God and having an increased expectation for the miraculous. There has been a renewed expectation of the moving of the Holy Spirit, signs and wonders as a part of daily life, prayer for physical healings with miracles recorded by YouTube videos, and heartfelt worship to God lifted up by the saints all around the globe.

However, notice in Matthew 22 when this first invitation was met with rejection, another was issued. It is my conviction that the Holy Spirit is once again sweeping through our cities but this time instead of within the walls of the church it is an invitation going out to everyone on the street corners, places of business, on college campuses, within prisons, among gang members, to those living in drug houses, and all across every neighborhood in every city to draw the lost to the Lord. In Luke 19:10, Jesus said, "For the Son of Man came to seek and to save that which was lost." For many years we've placed the emphasis on the fact He came to save the lost, but I believe we need to shift our thinking to the fact that He first is seeking the lost. If Jesus, the Head of the Church is seeking the lost, don't you think His Body, should be seeking to find them as well? Not only did Jesus come to seek and to save HE who was lost; He came to seek and to save THAT which was lost. It is the word "that" that appears in the Greek text of this verse and begs the question, "What was lost?" The answer is threefold: 1. Man lost his intimacy with God and God with man. Secondly, man lost his intimacy with his fellow man and thirdly, the whole garden was lost – the marketplace and center of the universe in Adam's day. It was the spiritual center (God walked with Adam and Eve there); it was the educational center (God conversed with Adam and Eve); it was the commercial center ("Be fruitful and multiply"); and it was a governmental center (authority of the highest level was present there). And God was involved in every area of life in the Garden of Eden and He is now seeking all "that" which is lost.

After working over twenty years inside the four walls of a non-denominational church to now working in my local police department, I am amazed at the number of people living in our communities who know nothing at all about God. I completely agree with a statement I've heard, "You no longer need a plane ticket to go to the mission field." Right in our own cities and neighborhoods, supermarkets, schools and businesses, people are hurting, tormented and so desperately in need of God's love. By working on a church staff and interacting with other churches for over two decades, I know most churches are filled with good-hearted people looking for ways to impact their communities. Traditional church growth strategies are where members are asked to invite people to come to church with them. The intent is those coming to church will experience a life change, begin to grow spiritually, be discipled and benefit from all the activities in the household of faith. This model has largely been my own wonderful church experience. Church leaders continue to look for new ways to conduct community outreach only to face barriers and the modern day misconception of the gospel being an unwanted message within the mainstream of our societal systems. This thinking creates closed doors and denies Christians access to having outreach programs or even mentioning faith inside most secular organizations or campuses.

There are more people than you might realize who have never even heard the gospel living in our cities and who have no concept at all of the purpose of "church." This includes people from the poorest to the wealthiest, and uneducated to the educated. Every Sunday there are plenty of other things for them to do instead of attending church. What I've experienced the past four years in my city are beyond anything I could have conceived being part of in 1977 while I was attending Rhema Bible Training Center. I now see my city in the way I think God sees it. It's no longer acceptable to me that there are those living around me who may die unsaved and live all of eternity separated from God. It is my hope that this book will encourage believers because wherever you live, your city is a lot like mine. God not only can, but strongly desires to use you in ways far beyond your own natural abilities to solve challenges facing your community. In doing so you will gain access to the hurting for the purpose of building relationships with all the people He is seeking to save. It is my conviction that the church understands Jesus saving the lost, but the church needs to understand the fact He is first seeking them. Hopefully, what I am sharing will serve as a road map, to point you toward possible unconventional ways for accessing the lost and unchurched. Not only are we seeking to find those who are lost but we are also seeking to restore all "that" which was lost. There are people in your community who are broken but some of the systems meant to assist them are struggling as well and God can work through you to bring the very solutions they are in need of. This road map can be replicated within every city in America and even many cities around the world. The infrastructure of cities everywhere is quite similar and though some of the organizations I'll discuss in later chapters might have different names in your town, nevertheless, these services exist and hopefully this book will help steer you to them.

God certainly loves the hurting much more than we do. He sent His Son from heaven to live on earth and then to die for them. Even if they don't know it yet, He is ready to welcome them into His family with opened arms. God also wants to solve your community's most challenging problems. He wants to alleviate suffering and abuse by empowering you with solutions, granting you favor to walk through doors that are now standing open all over your city. And there in your city, is where you will find hundreds and thousands who are hurting, confused, tormented and unchurched, ready to be reached with the love of God and the power of the gospel. Literally, the message I'm proclaiming is...YOUR CITY IS WAITING ON YOU!

Let these words stir the fires of compassion in your heart and ignite your imagination. Take this map and head in a new direction where you can boldly step out to serve others. Trust God to solve community problems you might learn about even if they are in areas where you have had no prior training or experience. Be encouraged to know God is with you. He has never intended that we work in the harvest fields without Him. Anywhere you take Him, He knows what to do.

One of my favorite places to hike in the mountains with my family is a park where there is a natural tunnel large enough for a train to pass through the mountain. The railroad actively uses it daily as a part their rail system. When you stand near the tunnel and face it, there is nothing but a rock wall all around it. However if you look closely at this rock wall, you will always find a few green plants pushing and growing their way through the hardness of the rock. It's quite amazing to see a green shoot with leaves sticking out of a rock wall. Seeing this always reminds me how God's life inside us can also grow anywhere, even through the hard places. He will actually send you into the hard places knowing that His Blessing will distinguish you there!

Do you know of any hard places around you? Maybe personally you are facing some rock hard challenges in your life or family? I'm certain there are some in your city. Challenges like high crime, rampant drug addiction, domestic violence, abuse, unemployment, teenagers dropping out of school, hunger, homelessness, prison overcrowding, human trafficking on the rise and the list goes on. Have you ever thought about God wanting to work through you to push through some of those "hard places?" When you were born again,

God put His nature on the inside of you. Limitations? There are none. God has promised to be with you.

James 1:5 says, "If any of you is deficient in wisdom, let him ask of the giving God [Who gives] to everyone liberally and ungrudgingly, without reproaching or faultfinding, and it will be given him." If you are a parent and want to know how to reach a stubborn teenager, do you know you can ask God for wisdom and He will give it to you? Along the same lines, do you know He also knows how to reduce prison overcrowding in your state and find solutions to overcoming the barriers for reentry into the community for those previously incarcerated? Have you ever thought to ask God how to do something like this? Have you ever walked in the shoes of someone who is facing barriers that keep them from breaking the cycle of crime in their lives? Or how about if your town needs mentors to walk alongside at-risk children and youth growing up in homes where parents are addicted to drugs or are incarcerated? Do you know God knows how to do that too and promises His favor will assist you as you join the efforts of local agencies and become a blessing to not only the children and youth you serve but the agency as well? If we lack wisdom about anything, God has the answer and is happy to share it with us if we will ask Him.

As we believe God's life is on the inside of us and we can access His wisdom, we will begin to see ourselves as a mighty force for change. In the Book of Acts 17:6, the early Christians were described as "these men who have turned the world upside down." More accurately I think they "turned it right side up" because darkness is behind all things that fail. God is the One who brings restoration and repair. But it was people that God used to bring this restoration. Are you willing to help turn your town "right side up?" You can do it because you have God living inside of you! Meditate on that truth and daily declare, "Greater is He who lives in you than he who is in the world." (1st John 4:4)

How can you grow more aware of God being inside you and God being with you? It's easy to think about God being with us on Sunday when we go to church or when we read our Bibles or in times of prayer, but what about when we are in a board room working on plans to finish a project within budget and it seems impossible? Do you think God knows how to bring the project within budget? Do you think He's willing to help you? I can tell you that His Word says He is with you, and in you, and is willing to help.

Throughout the Bible we find accounts where mighty deeds are accomplished by people who knew they had God with them. In Second Samuel 5:10 the prophet speaking of King David said, "David became greater and greater, for the Lord God of hosts was with him." Concerning Solomon, Second Chronicles 1:1 says, "Solomon son of David was strengthened in his kingdom and the Lord his God was with him and made him exceedingly great." When Joseph was falsely accused by Potiphar's wife and thrown into prison, "The prison ward paid no attention to anything that was in Joseph's charge, for the Lord was with him and made whatever he did to prosper." (Genesis 39:23) Even in the ministry of Jesus, it was noted in Act 10:38 that the mighty deeds He did were attributed to the fact that God was with Him. "How God anointed and consecrated Jesus of Nazareth with the Holy Spirit and with strength and ability and power, how He went about doing good and, in particular, curing all who were harassed and oppressed by the power of the devil, for God was with Him." Before Jesus ascended into heaven to be seated at the right hand of His Father, He told the disciples "Instruct them in the practice of all I have commanded you. I'll be with you as you do this, day after day after day, right up to the end of the age." (Matthew 28:20 The Message Bible) Every single day, day after day until the end of the church age we can be assured He will be with us! Not only is He with us, but through us He is compelling the lost to come into the Kingdom from the highways, out on street corners, inside public schools, prisons, and housing developments.

It is my purpose to show you how very easy it is to access those who are hurting through doors already standing open. Jesus came to seek and to save those who are lost. He is with you and is still seeking them but now He is using you. The harvest all around you is abundant and it is ripe. Are you ready to go out into your town and seek those who need Him? He has equipped you for extraordinary tasks and will be with you to complete them. He does not call you based upon your own abilities. He has made available His Blessing for you. This Blessing will be at work wherever you go and whatever you undertake. God values most your availability because He is full of ability and eager to share it with you.

GOD'S SUPER ADDED TO YOUR NATURAL

"The blessing of the Lord—it makes [truly] rich, and He adds no sorrow with it [neither does toiling increase it]."

(Proverbs 10:22)

Imagine scientists and engineers who are employed by the space program trying to launch a capsule into outer space hoping to have it land on the moon but by doing so without the aid of any rocket boosters. Once mission control performed the countdown, this highly advanced aircraft would not accomplish what it had been designed and tested to do without the help of an explosive force thrusting it heavenward provided by the rockets attached to it. Over the course of my life I have watched by television several missions as they lifted off from the Kennedy Space Center in Florida. As a child I remember the whole family gathering around the television to watch and to listen to the nightly news, hearing the voices of astronauts from outer space. When I was eleven years old I saw the images on TV and heard the words from astronauts live as they took their first walk on the moon. These historical events would never have been accomplished without the help of the rockets that powered them to their space destinations.

In a similar way, do you know God never designed for you to fulfill your mission in life without having His powerful help? In Ephesians 2:10 it says, "For we are God's [own] handiwork (His workmanship), recreated in Christ Jesus, [born anew] that we may do those good works which God predestined (planned beforehand) for us [taking paths which He prepared ahead of time], that we should walk in them [living the good life which He prearranged and made ready for us to live]." Similar to how scientists and engineers created the highly sophisticated space capsule to travel to the moon, you have been created by God. Not only created by Him but given a Divine mission to fulfill. God never intended that we fulfill our life mission without the explosive force of His empowerment. From the beginning of mankind, it has always been God's desire to bless us with a heavenly empowerment which He calls "The Blessing." Since the word "blessing" is so casually used in our vocabulary, I'm going to capitalize the word when I refer to it in this section. My reason for doing this is to impress upon your thinking that it's HUGE! This Blessing is from God! It signifies that God is with us. It is His anointing and empowerment for our lives to carry out tasks that we could never accomplish alone by relying on our own wisdom, strength or ability.

Two places we can see God's will and desire for man coming to pass completely unhindered by the opposition of the enemy are in Heaven and in the Garden of Eden. In Heaven, the book of Revelation 21:4 describes conditions where, "God will wipe away every tear from their eyes; and death shall be no more, neither shall there be anguish (sorrow and mourning) nor grief nor pain any more, for the old conditions and the former order of things have passed away." There is constant worship of God around His throne, and there is no sickness, death or even crying. The other place is in the Garden of Eden at Creation. In Genesis 1:26-28 we read, "God said, Let Us [Father, Son, and Holy Spirit] make mankind in Our image, after Our likeness, and let them have complete authority over the fish of the sea, the birds of the air, the [tame] beasts, and over all of the earth, and over everything that creeps upon the earth. So God created man in His own image, in the image *and* likeness of God He created him; male and female He created them. And God blessed them and said to them, Be fruitful, multiply, and fill the earth, and subdue it [using all its vast resources in the service of God and man]; and have dominion over the fish of the sea, the birds of the air, and over every living creature that moves upon the earth." God the Father, Son and Holy Spirit were all present as God created Adam and Eve then breathed life into them. The very first words out of God's mouth at the sight of these two are ones of blessings over them. Being a parent myself, I understand the overwhelming aspiration to bring nothing but good upon my children from the first moment I ever laid eyes on them. No parent would ever desire harm, sickness, calamity or even disappointment for their children. Why then would we think God does for His children? If you follow through the book of Genesis after the fall of man, immediately God is right back at work initiating a way to connect His Blessing to mankind through a covenant with Abraham. It seems blessing is always on God's mind where mankind is concerned. Anywhere we find mankind failing, God has a one track mind towards restoring His Blessing back to them again.

In Deuteronomy 15, we read where God entered into a covenant with Abram. Abram was his name before God changed it in Genesis 17:5 to Abraham. The covenant was accomplished by God putting Abram to sleep, indicating that He took care of all the work. What a beautiful picture of our salvation. It's not by our own works, or we would boast! In Deuteronomy 28:1-13 we find God defining for Abram what the blessing is and later in the same chapter what the curse is. God removes all doubt what each are by distinguishing between The Blessing and the curse. The Blessing could have consisted of anything since God decided the parameters of what it would include. The Blessing came by obedience, and the curse came by disobedience. In these verses we read The Blessing described as an amazing endowment of the goodness of God. "If you will listen diligently to the voice of the Lord your God, being watchful to do all His commandments which I command you this day, the Lord your God will set you high above all the nations of the earth. And all these blessings shall come upon you and overtake you if you heed the voice of the Lord your God. Blessed shall you be in the city and blessed shall you be in the field. Blessed shall be the fruit of your body and the fruit of your ground and the fruit of your beasts, the increase of your cattle and the young of your flock. Blessed shall be your basket and your kneading trough. Blessed shall you be when you come in and blessed shall you be when you go out. The Lord shall cause your enemies who rise up against you to be defeated before your face; they shall come out against you one way and flee before you seven ways. The Lord shall command the blessing upon you in your storehouse and in all that you undertake. And He will bless you in the land which the Lord your God gives you. The Lord will establish you as a people holy to Himself, as He has sworn to you, if you keep the commandments of the Lord your God and walk in His ways. And all people of the earth shall see that you are called by the name [and in the presence of] the Lord, and they shall be afraid of you. And the Lord shall make you have a surplus of prosperity, through the fruit of your body, of your livestock, and of your ground, in the land which the Lord swore to your fathers to give you. The Lord shall open to you His good treasury, the heavens, to give the rain of your land in its season and to bless all the work of your hands; and you shall lend to many nations, but you shall not borrow. And the Lord shall make you the head, and not the tail; and you shall be above only, and you shall not be beneath, if you heed the commandments of the Lord your God which I command you this day and are watchful to do them."

The Blessing upon a man was designed to give him extreme advantage. God allows us to be part of the amazing work that He is doing in the earth in order to draw people to Him. Just like the space capsule lifts off with the explosive help of the rocket boosters, God has equipped us with a powerful advantage. Let this passage of scripture in Deuteronomy become a reality to you. Read it over verse by verse. Write it down. Meditate on it. Imagine what it would be like to be blessed coming in and blessed going out or as we would say today, whether you are coming or going – you are blessed! Consider having an enemy come against you in one way, but with God's anointing upon you, it would be scattered and run away in seven ways! This would be like a scene out of a superhero movie. God said His Blessing will cause people to be in awe of you, which is for the sake of drawing them to Him. In effect, He will increase your sphere of influence beyond anything you could do in the natural. He will raise you up. You don't have to raise yourself up – His anointing upon you knows how to do it. He will make you to have a surplus of goods and make you the head (out in front) and not the tail (underneath). This Blessing is simply defined as God's "Super" upon our "Natural." His rocket added to our space capsule! It is an amazing thing that where ever we go or whatever we do, The Blessing will work for us if we believe that it will. What a perfect heavenly advantage!

Throughout the Old Testament we read where the firstborn in the family received the father's coveted blessing. The Blessing was considered an endowment or guarantee of success that operated wherever the firstborn went and whatever he undertook. Genesis 13:1-16 records a perfect illustration of the blessing at work in the life of Abram. There came a time when he, his wife and Lot left Egypt and traveled into Bethel. In verses 6-9 we read, "Now the land was not able to nourish and support them (both Lot and Abram) so they could dwell together, for their possessions were too great for them to live together. So Abram said to Lot, 'Let there be no strife, I beg of you, between you and me or between your herdsmen and my herdsmen, for we are relatives. Is not the whole land before you? Separate yourself, I beg of you, from me. If you take the left hand, then I will go to the right; or if you choose the right hand, then I will go to the left."

Why was Abram so confident that whichever land Lot chose, the remaining land left for him to settle his herds on would still flourish? Because he knew he had God's Blessing! God had told him His blessing is working whether you are coming in or going out, and it works if you are in the field or in the city. Abram knew it would work on whatever or wherever he put his hand to. When we accept this truth about God's Blessing on our lives, we should refuse to be limited by thinking that says we cannot succeed because we are not from the right family, or politically connected enough, or have the right education, or of the right gender or ethnicity. With God's Blessing, none of these things can hold you back unless you believe that they can! Abram knew wherever he would make his home that God's blessing would be with him for increase. That's exactly what he experienced. When I came to work at the police department, the objectives I was given to accomplish seemed beyond what I knew I could do. However, I trusted that God had promised to be with me and help me whether I was in the "city" or in the field.

In Genesis chapters 37, 39-46 we read about the life of Joseph. Joseph was a dreamer who told his brothers his dream of seeing them all bowing down before him. He was also highly favored by Jacob their father who gave him a coat of many colors as a sign of his love for Joseph. His jealous, enraged brothers wanted to kill him. Instead, after throwing him into a pit, they decided to sell him to slave traders, telling their father that a wild animal had devoured him. Joseph was brought down to Egypt where Potiphar, an officer of Pharaoh, the captain and chief executioner of the royal guard bought him from the Ishmaelite slave traders. (Genesis 39:1) Even in these difficult circumstances for him, we see in verses 2-4, "The Lord was with Joseph, and he though a slave was a successful and prosperous man; and he was in the house of his master the Egyptian. And his master saw that the Lord was with him and that the Lord made all that he did to flourish and succeed in his hand. So Joseph pleased Potiphar and found favor in his sight, and he served him. And his master made him supervisor over his house and put all that he had in his charge."

Before Joseph went to live with Potiphar, we have no indication that Joseph had ever managed anything. But here in the home of this high ranking officer, because of The Blessing, Joseph not only excelled in whatever he was to manage, he did it so well that Potiphar recognized God was with Joseph. Doesn't that sound like the results of The Blessing as described in Deuteronomy 28? Whatever he did prospered! The Blessing on our lives is to be a sign to the unbelieving.

As time goes on, Potiphar's wife tried to seduce Joseph, but instead he acted nobly and ran away, yet she lied about him to Potiphar. As a result Joseph was sent to prison. (Genesis 39:6-20) But even being in prison could not stop The Blessing! Verses 21-23 says, "But the Lord was with Joseph, and showed him mercy and loving-kindness and gave him favor in the sight of the warden of the prison. And the warden of the prison committed to Joseph's care all the prisoners who were in the prison; and whatsoever was done there, he was in charge of it. The prison warden paid no attention to anything that was in Joseph's charge, for the Lord was with him and made whatever he did to prosper." Once again we see that The Blessing God gave to Abraham caused Joseph to excel in prison to the point that the warden put him in charge of running the place. Whatever he put his hand to, God blessed it! Wherever he went, God caused him to flourish! I know a little bit about prisons. For all those incarcerated, you have to provide all the meals, medical care, laundry and every single detail for sustaining life. It's likely that the prison system in Joseph's day was far less comfortable than conditions today, but it still required organization and management skills to operate this facility and it was The Blessing which empowered Joseph to do it.

In the book of Daniel we read where Daniel and three Hebrews were taken into the house of the Babylonian king Nebuchadnezzar. These young men underwent training in literature and the language of the Chaldeans. (Daniel 1:4) In Daniel 1:9 the Bible says, "Now God made Daniel to find favor, compassion and loving-kindness with the chief of the eunuchs." In other words Daniel had God's Blessing upon him that gave him an advantage. In verse 20 we find when the time came for Daniel and the three Hebrews to be tested in the matters of wisdom and understanding, the king found them to be ten times better than all the others within his whole kingdom. It was The Blessing that caused these four young men to stand out so significantly. Daniel and the three Hebrews after being examined by the king's staff were found to be not just one or two times better but ten times better because God was with them!

Proverbs 10:22 says, "The blessing of the Lord – it makes [truly] rich, and He adds no sorrow with it [neither does toiling increase it.]" This verse delineates that The Blessing is not of our own doing, and all our efforts or works will not improve it. It has nothing to do with our personality, talents or training. We need to see ourselves as God with us, His empowerment rests upon us and it covers over every part of our life. His anointing knows how to get any job done, and our toiling does not increase it or make it more effective. This doesn't mean God is opposed to us working hard but it's not our toiling that makes us Blessed. If this was the case then it would not be by grace and the free favor of God. If we had to do anything to earn or deserve it then some could be disqualified, but the good news of the gospel is that none are disqualified. God loves you, and there is nothing you can do about it! The Blessing is upon all who are His. All we do is believe it and then expect it to be at work on our behalf. A great indicator that The Blessing is all about God's provision and not about our own self effort is found in Psalm 127. In verse 2 it says, "It is vain for you to rise up early, to take rest late, to eat the bread of [anxious] toil-for He gives [blessings] to His beloved in sleep." This verse paints the picture that it's God's desire for us to have sweat less victory! There have been times in my life when I've been concerned about a presentation I had to make at work the next day so I stayed up late working on it worriedly making changes and then again woke up before dawn anxious if it would be effective. But since, I've come to lean on The Blessing, now I just do my best to prepare and then rest.

Do you know The Blessing as described in the Old Testament has never been rescinded? It has no shelf-life expiration date. The Blessing rests upon you today as a child of God. Each of us needs to become "Blessing minded." Make it a habit to meditate on Deuteronomy 28:1-13 and declare it over your life. Write it down verse by verse and like steps on a ladder comprehend what each verse is telling you God so graciously wants to do for you. You will begin to be like David when he took on Goliath. Instead of running away from this giant who was threatening the army of Israel, he ran towards him! When you are armed with The Blessing of God, you know any problem is no match for Him! You might say, "Well, The Blessing is just for those living under the Old Testament." Not so! Galatians 3:14 says, "To the end that through their receiving Christ Jesus, The Blessing promised to Abraham might come upon the Gentiles, so that we through faith might all receive the realization of the promise of the Holy Spirit." Have you received Christ Jesus as your Lord and Savior? If the answer is yes, then the promised Blessing of Abraham has come upon you! Expect The Blessing to increase you in every way. The Blessing will teach you and help you understand things you've not had any experience in. It will not only teach you but then raise you up to excel in these areas. His Blessing will fill your heart, mind and imagination with solutions to challenges faced within your sphere of professional influence. His Blessing and anointing will expand your creativity and release potential in you far beyond your own natural abilities. Expect that whatever image The Blessing puts inside of you, it will also take you to a place where it can be expressed. You will see God direct your steps to the right place just at the right time. And the best part is that like Daniel and the three Hebrews, you can experience being ten times better in an area than those without The Blessing. You may find yourself teaching the experts in a field because God has given you a more efficient, cost effective way to produce results. I have experienced this. The Blessing is His Super upon your natural!

In the New Testament the Apostle Paul immediately, after his conversion begins to preach the gospel. "But Saul increased all the more in strength, and continued to confound the Jews who lived in Damascus by comparing and examining evidence and proving that Jesus is the Christ the Messiah." (Acts. 9:22) Given his background as the chief persecutor of the church this is quite amazing! We read in Acts chapter 7 that Stephen was preaching the gospel when "they raised a great shout and put their hands over their ears and rushed together upon him. They dragged him out of the city and began to stone him, and the witnesses placed their garments at the feet of a young man named Saul." (Acts 7:57-58) So in the short span of only two chapters we see Saul going from zealously trying to stop the preaching of the gospel, even approving of the stoning of Stephen, to now preaching the gospel himself. What a huge contrast! If ever someone needed God's Super upon their natural it was the Apostle Paul. Though he was an educated man and naturally very gifted, he spent years using these gifts to silence the very message he later came to love and promote. In the Book of Ephesians, as he's writing a letter to the church in the city of Ephesus, chapter 3 describes how it was God who equipped him. "This is my life work: helping people understand and respond to this Message. It came as a sheer gift to me, a real surprise, God handling all the details. When it came to presenting the Message to people who had no background in God's way, I was the least qualified of any of the available Christians. God saw to it that I was equipped, but you can be sure that it had nothing to do with my natural abilities. And so here I am, preaching and writing about things that are way over my head, the inexhaustible riches and generosity of Christ. My task is to bring out in the open and make plain what God, who created all this in the first place, has been doing in secret and behind the scenes all along." (Ephesians 3:7-9 The Message Bible)

In my work at the police department my grant specified that one of the four initiatives the team was required to address was an offender intervention that would reduce recidivism. I knew I could count on The Blessing of God and He was with me at work. Within the first 30 days on the job, a corrections manager suggested to me that we travel to another state to visit a probation program she thought was similar to what we were considering creating as our offender intervention. Unbeknownst to any of us, on the exact day and time we visited that program; a woman who was a national expert in reducing recidivism was on site conducting a program audit for a federal agency. This woman was very knowledgeable in reducing recidivism. In addition, she had worked with some of the leading experts in this field from other states. She had co-authored and published journal articles for best practices regarding working with this population. From the moment I met her and shared what we hoped to create in our town, God gave me tremendous favor with her. For almost 6 months she arranged her schedule to attend planning meetings of the development team and coached us all along the way. She joined us when meeting with judges, mental health and corrections personnel guiding us into evidenced-based practices for reducing recidivism. When we started developing the program, she and other corrections directors would text me the proper phrases to use when communicating with the judges for describing concepts we were introducing. However, in only a matter of a few months after hearing me speak to a group one day, one of our corrections directors said, "I'm amazed how quickly you've grasped all this and can communicate it to others having no criminal justice background." Why was this so? It was because of The Blessing on my life. However, I wasn't only learning to speak knowledgeably about the need for states to reduce recidivism or the barriers that exist to community reentry; I also was growing to become a passionate advocate for this population.

When it became necessary to hire a manager of the program, God brought across my path someone who was a perfect fit. She became as determined as I was that the program would not fail. She was amazingly organized and resourceful, and thankfully a Christian, so many of the hurdles we faced we would commit to prayer. As we began to build the program we needed additional staff but had no funds to pay for them. So I went out into the community to talk with various organizations about our new program and asked them to get involved. During the period of development we experienced so much of God's favor that one by one, agencies began to get on board as partners. I called to schedule an appointment to meet with the CEO of a national agency who provides employment readiness training and assistance with online job searching. We were seeking a partner to provide employment training for individuals in the program, thinking it would be great if they just sent a trainer a few days a week to help. Instead when we met, he responded that though this service was not something they currently offered, their company would fund a position fully dedicated entirely to our program. This left the door open for us to craft a position into the exact standard we needed! Glory to God!

Over and over as this program took shape, the Lord reminded me it was His enablement and favor that we were experiencing at work. Think about the odds naturally. Without even knowing what kind of criminal justice expert was needed to help guide our offender program into becoming a reality, and not anticipating we would soon create a model that needed more staff than we could afford – the odds rather were against us. However, every single resource was revealed to make it work. It was clear to me that God's favor was with me! It was His Super upon my natural.

Over the three-year duration of the project, the probation program continued to flourish. One of my final responsibilities as Director was to secure funding to sustain all the programs we had created. Of the 19 programs, not many were costly and were very easily integrated into the community. However the probation program had an annual budget of around one hundred and thirty thousand dollars. I wrote two large grants during 2015 hoping to be awarded funding that would include sustaining this program for a few more years; however neither application was selected for funding. All the while I knew if God's Blessing and favor had helped me to create this program, He also had a way to fund it.

One day I was at the probation program to attend a staff meeting, when a corrections director who had been a member of my development team and also worked at this same location, called me into a room where she was meeting with someone from the state department of corrections. For almost an hour the person from the state asked me about the program and proposed to me sending information regarding it to the State Commissioner of corrections and to request funding for it after the grant ended. When I left that meeting,

I felt it had all been prearranged to have that discussion. Once again it was God that created this opportunity since I'd never seen or met this person prior to that time and now they were coaching me on how to obtain funding from the state.

Following that discussion, I enlisted the help of my state grant manager on how to propose to the department of corrections a request for funding. He suggested we provide with our request a cost benefit study of the program. We worked for weeks to collect all the data that was requested. Then my manager figured up the cost of someone attending our probation program comparing it to the cost for the state of an individual being incarcerated. We knew the program was operating economically because of all the in-kind community partners who provided their services but we had no idea HOW economically it was until the study was completed. The other piece I obtained to go along with our funding request that proved to be significant was a letter of support from the criminal court judge who made the largest number of client referrals to the program. When the judge sent me his letter, he had written to the commissioner that one hundred percent of those that he referred to the probation program would have been sent back to prison if not for this new and valuable resource.

Along with the judge's recommendations, we could demonstrate the savings of paying only twelve dollars per day for someone who was enrolled in our program compared to the cost of seventy-four dollars a day for that same person to be in prison. Not only was it a reduced cost to the state, but we were providing these individuals with education and therapy for drug addiction, relapse prevention, life and job skill training, anger management and individual counseling for one year - many of the tools they need to get back on their feet. Sending this information to the Commissioner of State Corrections along with our funding request brought a quick response from him indicating an interest in sustaining the program permanently after my grant ended, which they did. Not only did the state fund the program but they are now replicating it across the state! Within the first year after my grant ended, the Department of Corrections opened five centers statewide, and proposes more to come. When I look back I know without a doubt it was The Blessing upon my life that led me every step of the way to facilitate the development of a program to reduce recidivism that the Department of Corrections now funds and is replicating in other cities. What a picture of God adding His Super to my natural and how His favor assisted me every step of the way!

YOU HAVE AN ASSISTANT

"By the blessing of the influence of the upright and
God's favor [because of them] the city is exalted, but
it is overthrown by the mouth of the wicked."

(Proverbs 11:11)

For many years one area of interest in my personal Bible Study was learning about the favor of God. In the early years of my Christian walk, quality Bible study time required spreading out across my kitchen table several versions of the Bible, commentaries, Bible dictionaries and concordances. Thankfully in the past several years all that has been replaced by efficient Bible search engines online. With these you can type in the word or verse you want to study and select several options for viewing information related to it all with a few clicks of the keyboard.

In the spring of 2012 I decided to conduct an in-depth study on God's favor so I searched the word online and chose to locate its uses within the Amplified Bible and found there were 326 verses that included the word favor. I then printed all these off and put them in a notebook where I could read and meditate on them daily which I did for several months. Beside many of the verses I made notes of what that verse indicated the favor of God could do. Beginning in Genesis

12:2 when God was telling Abraham what would happen when He entered into covenant with him; God described the outcome in this way. "And I will make of you a great nation, and I will bless you with an abundant increase of favors and make your name famous and distinguished and you will be a blessing dispensing good to others." What a wonderful truth this revealed at the very start of my study that God's favor upon my life was to make me a "blessing dispensing good to others." When I saw this, I said, "Lord I accept this as true about me!" To give to others is more blessed than to receive, and here God was saying His favor was a vehicle to make that happen. So in my notebook beside this verse I wrote, "God's favor upon me is for me to be a blessing to others by dispensing good to them," and then I meditated on what that would look like.

As I read from verse to verse, most always looking them up in the context of what was going on before and after the verse in the chapter, it became clear to me that having God's favor was the same as Him giving me an Assistant to accomplish anything He's called me to do. What is the role of an "assistant?" For many years my husband has worked as a finish carpenter where he installs cabinetry in kitchens, baths and offices commercially and residentially. Because these can be very heavy, his company sends along an assistant to the job site to help him carry in the cabinets and assist him while he is mounting them. What is the purpose of this? It's to make the job easier! Without an assistant, many of the jobs would be impossible to undertake alone. But with an assistant along the end result is a beautiful kitchen or bathroom. In the same way, we need assistance to accomplish the plan of God for our lives. In order to make our jobs easier, God has given us His favor as an assistant.

Even though I had studied God's favor before, I decided to take a more in-depth look; this additional study transformed my thinking and increased my desire to learn the many ways favor can be expressed. Before this time, it had never occurred to me, when I was faced with certain kinds of challenges that I could expect God's favor to change the outcome. In Genesis 26:12 when the covenant people of God were experiencing a great famine, "Isaac sowed seed in that land and received in the same year a hundred times as much as he had planted, and the Lord favored him with blessings." From this, I learned that, "Favor does not quit working even in famine." Often when faced with obstacles and challenges, those we count on the most might disappoint us, but not so with the favor of God as favor does not quit under hardship. In Genesis 30 we find the story of Jacob working for Laban for seven years to earn the hand of his daughter Rachel in marriage. Instead, Laban deceives him and gives Jacob his daughter Leah. Finally, after another seven years, Jacob is given the hand of Rachel. Though Laban deceives Jacob, it was obvious that having Jacob as an employee had increased his wealth greatly. In verse 30 Jacob says to Laban, "For you had little before I came, and it was increased and multiplied abundantly; and the Lord has favored you with blessings wherever I turned." I noted with this verse that, "favor on my life will cause increase to come to those I work for." Think about that! You might be working in an industry that is struggling but if you grab hold of the fact that the favor of God upon you can bring increase to others, it can turn the situation around. Trust God that His favor upon you will show you solutions to challenges faced by your company.

This truth helped me as we were looking for ways to reduce crime in our Downtown. It is not uncommon in cities that the vibrancy once known to the downtown areas has been replaced by new shopping malls spread all across towns. Countless cities have tried new and innovative ways to revitalize their downtown and, in doing so; found that the older parts of town are where crime is now entrenched. With grant dollars we were able to utilize off duty officers coming in to work special patrols. These officers worked extra patrols concentrating in areas where certain types of crime most frequently occurred. As I learned that God's favor upon my life could bring increase to those I worked for, it caused me to have daily expectancy that solutions to some of the challenges faced by our department would become evident to me. I had heard residents and merchants comment about how dark certain blocks of town were, so the idea came to me to search the crime data to see what "time of day" crime occurred the most. This study revealed that in the residential neighborhood we were focusing our efforts on, crime was highest late in the evening between midnight and 1 a.m. before it dropped off significantly. Reviewing the data for the Downtown areas, I saw a whole different story. For the Downtown areas the greatest numbers of calls for service were happening between 2-4 a.m. due to the fact that area bars closed at 3 a.m. While discussing this finding with the Sergeant who worked with us on scheduling overtime patrols, he commented that normally this extra shift had been ending at 2 a.m. As a result, he started extending shifts to 4 a.m. In one six-month period we had 64 additional arrests for drug-related activities and public intoxication because we had the proactive presence of officers Downtown during those extended hours.

In Genesis 39, we read where Joseph has been sold by his jealous brothers and now became a slave to Poitphar, the chief executioner in the Royal Guard of Pharaoh. In verse 4 it says, "So Joseph pleased Potiphar and found favor in his sight and he served him. And his master made him supervisor over his house and he put all that he had in his charge." Favor is your assistant and will bring you into places of management where you will be given greater responsibility. We can expect God's wisdom to flow through our lives daily. We need to be like David when he confronted the giant Goliath - don't run from challenges but instead run towards them. What challenge could you possibly face in life or out in the marketplace that God doesn't know the solution to?

In Exodus 3, God had chosen Moses to lead His people out of Egypt, where they had suffered years of hardship and slavery, into the Promised Land. In verse 21 God said to Moses, "I will give this people favor and respect in the sight of the Egyptians; and it shall be that when you go, you shall not go empty-handed." Let's stop a minute and think about this situation. Four hundred years, the children of Israel worked for Pharaoh. In fact, Pharaoh hated God's people so much so that he made their workloads unreasonable. It was his hope that their women worked so hard they would not be able to physically conceive children. Commonly, they were beaten and despised and deprived of food. But as they were departing, God tells Moses that because of His favor, they are to ask the Egyptians for their belongings and they will just hand them over. There is no other way this would have happened without God's favor. How amazing is it to think that favor can reverse someone's attitude towards us from hatred to the position of them handing over to us their belongings! Or we could say favor changed their attitude from making life hard for us to a position of aiding us.

Leviticus 26:9 says, speaking of God, "I will be leaning toward you with favor and regard for you, rendering you fruitful, multiplying you, and establishing and ratifying My covenant with you." How many situations do we find ourselves in where it would make a recognizable difference by knowing that the favor of God will assist the outcome to our advantage? Near the end of my grant I received a commitment from the State Department of Corrections confirming that they would fund the probation program effective April 1st. However, in January of that year, I received a phone call from an Assistant Commissioner. He informed me that the State Comptroller conveyed that funding could not begin until July 1st when the new fiscal year began. Prior to this, it had been indicated that coverage would begin effective April 1st at the end of our grant and would cover the three months prior to the new fiscal year beginning in July. As a result of this new information, I would need to identify about thirty-thousand dollars to fill this gap. Months before, when the state indicated they would sustain the program, I had ceased looking for any grants or other forms of funding and now the clock was ticking. Remembering the verse in Leviticus 26 where I was promised outcomes leaning in my favor, I decided to trust God's assistance instead of panicking. After all, where would I find thirty-thousand dollars on my own? I decided to call to the organization that was funding my entire project to share this recent development. My thought was that they may be able to offer some suggestions regarding where to solicit three months of additional funding. Surprisingly, my grant manager replied, "we'll give you additional funding to cover the three months deficit." With one phone call, which lasted less than 10 minutes, the project received an extension of an additional thirty-thousand dollars.

One of the most important benefits of realizing God's favor is to understand that it is an indicator of His constant love for you. I enjoy doing favors for people that are dear to me, often in the form of cooking a meal for them. Over the years I have grown to have a reputation for this. I've cooked countless meals for friends when new babies were born, or when family members were hospitalized, or even had passed away. I guess you could say I loved them with food. On the other hand I appreciate being the recipient of favors from others, as well. When my sons were young, there were some situations that would arise where my regular child care would fall through at the last moment. Having responsibilities at work, I'd call a good friend, who I knew I could ask a favor of and even though she had children of her own she would still help me. Why was I confident that she would help me? It was because of the closeness of my relationship with her. It's amazing to know that God desires our success so much so that He would help us in whatever task is before us. Understanding that God wants to show us His unearned favors is quite humbling and amazing at the same time. Over the years I've realized that it doesn't matter what the challenge involves or even the subject matter, He knows how to solve it!

Esther is a great example of someone who experienced the favor of God. One place in particular is found in Esther chapter 8. Haman had devised an evil plot against the Jews and had tricked King Ahasuerus into signing it into law. In verse 5 Esther comes before the king to ask if this decree could be reversed. "And she said, If it pleases the king and if I have found favor in his sight and the thing seems right before the king and I am pleasing in his eyes, let it be written to reverse the letters devised by Haman son of Hammedatha, the Agagite, which he wrote to destroy the Jews who are in the king's province." Just a few verses later, we are told that the King favored Esther and reversed his decree against the Jews. Are you facing an unfavorable decree against you? God's favor can reverse this decree if you put your trust in Him and accept His assistance.

When we first started the probation program, the funding required that the monies be spent on reducing crime and recidivism in only two neighborhoods. This stipulation meant that if someone was going to be referred from court to our program, the Program Manager had to research arrest records to determine if an individual either committed a felony inside one of these two neighborhoods or they were living in one of the neighborhoods. After about six months of operating this way, it became apparent this limitation was frustrating to the judges as they tried to identify candidates to refer to the program. Once again I contacted my grant manager but this time to request the referral boundaries be increased outside of these two neighborhoods to include the whole county. Doing this would make it easier for referrals to be made as well as increase the number of individuals who could benefit from the program. Initially my request was received unfavorably since the original contract approval specified all the services had to be focused within the geographical area noted in our grant application. In the days that ensued waiting for a final decision to be handed down, the story of Esther came to mind. Esther also required a decision to be reversed against her people - the Jews. Remembering that God's favor is what reversed that decree, my faith began to rise! I began to pray that we would also have favor for reversal of the decision in order for more people to benefit from the resources our probation program offered. Within a few days, I received an email noting these exact words, "We have reversed our original decision in order to allow you to accept referrals from outside the two neighborhoods. We are extending the referral boundaries to cover the whole area of the county in which the court resides." That's favor! Similar to God's favor on Esther, thereby saving her nation, we witnessed His favor in saving our program!

Proverbs 11:11 says, "By the blessing of the influence of the up-right and God's favor [because of them] the city is exalted, but it is overthrown by the mouth of the wicked." By continually thanking God for using my life to cause our city to be exalted in some way, I believe He will. On two occasions delegations visited our city to increase their knowledge of our crime reduction programs. One group was from another town in our state which is almost three times the size of our town; the other delegation was from a neighboring state. This verse says by God's favor and blessing upon you, your whole city can be exalted. As noted in this scripture, it is apparent that having these visitors is a reflection of the influence of the upright and our city being exalted.

There are other examples in the Bible of all-encompassing ways, in which favor will work for you like an assistant. These accounts in scripture are to illustrate how God has predetermined to show us His favor, and they serve as practical ways, in which they can be demonstrated in our lives. God's favor can make any job easier. However these examples are not only for work-related matters. Expect God's favor to help you in marriage, raising your children, buying a home and everything that relates to an abundant life. Determine today to expect an increase of God's favor towards you. God is in love with you, and He wants for you to experience His assistance. Not only does He love you, but He also greatly loves those with whom you come in contact. He wants to show them His love, by working through you. God is revealing the knowledge of His goodness all over the earth. By what means is He accomplishing this? By our simply determining to serve others everywhere we go. Remember God is not looking for your ability but He is seeking your availability.

THE GREATEST MINISTRY OF ALL

"Whoever wants to be great must become a servant.
Whoever wants to be first among you must be your slave."

Jesus (Mark 10:44 Message Bible)

You do not have to be a Christian very long to realize that God's ways are not the ways of the world. In the world it's "dog eat dog" with people pushing their way to the front of the line or in traffic. Growing up I don't remember hearing on news reports about "road rage" or public displays of anger by people unleashed through tragic events like school and mall shootings. In Second Timothy chapter three, we find an apt description of the days we are living in now. "But understand this, that in the last days will come (set in) perilous times of great stress and trouble [hard to deal with and hard to bear]. For people will be lovers of self and [utterly] self-centered, lovers of money and aroused by an inordinate [greedy] desire for wealth, proud and arrogant and contemptuous boasters. They will be abusive (blasphemous, scoffing), disobedient to parents, ungrateful, unholy and profane. [They will be] without natural [human] affection (callous and inhuman), relentless (admitting of no truce or appeasement); [they will be] slanderers (false accusers, troublemakers), intemperate and loose in morals and conduct, uncontrolled and fierce, haters of good. [They will be] treacherous [betrayers], rash, [and] inflated with self-conceit. [They will be] lovers of sensual pleasures and vain amusements more than and rather than lovers of God." (2 Timothy 3:1-4). What an accurate image of the selfish and abusive generation we are now living in. It's not uncommon to see images of parents slumped over in a car, passed out, as a result of drug addiction while their children are strapped in car seats. As a parent it's hard for me to comprehend this kind of negligence. It is not uncommon to see tempers flaring over varying political views, even over simple things like a high school ballgame or at a shopping mall where people rudely push to the front of lines with little regard for anyone who might have been there first. This passage in Timothy depicts people in the last days living selfish, self-indulging, ungrateful, uncontrolled lifestyle so as Christians; we are called to walk by a much higher standard.

Ten of the disciples once grew indignant because James and John requested of Jesus that they be seated beside Him in His glory. Mark 10:42-45 tells us, "But Jesus called them to Him and said to them, You know that those who are recognized as governing and are supposed to rule the Gentiles the nations lord it over them [ruling with absolute power, holding them in subjection], and their great men exercise authority and dominion over them. But this is not to be so among you: instead, whoever desires to be great among you must be your servant, And whoever wishes to be most important and first in rank among you must be slave of all. For even the Son of Man came not to have service rendered to Him, but to serve, and to give His life as a ransom for (instead of) many." Jesus witnessed James and John and He shared with them the need to choose to serve others. As a matter of fact, Jesus told the disciples whoever wanted to be great in the kingdom needed to be a servant. In John chapter 13, Jesus beautifully portrays serving others when He washed the feet of His disciples. However Jesus' identity, as a servant, started long before this humble exercise.

When Jesus came to earth He taught us that being a servant is not merely a set of actions but it is a mindset and a choice. Philippians

2:5-8, in the Message Bible, says, "Think of yourselves in the way Christ Jesus thought of himself. He had equal status with God but didn't think so much of himself that he had to cling to the advantages of that status no matter what. Not at all. When the time came, he set aside the privileges of Deity and took on the status of a slave, became human! Having become human, he stayed human. It was an incredibly humbling process. He didn't claim special privileges. Instead, he lived a selfless, obedient life and then died a selfless, obedient death – and the worst kind of death at that – a crucifixion." I don't believe in this life, that we are able to fully grasp what it meant for Jesus to humble Himself, leave heaven as the Son of God and come to earth as a man. This passage in Philippians explains that when Jesus left heaven, He left behind His deity privileges. Once He came to earth, He gave up His right to presume that if things weren't going very well that He could just say, "Okay, I think I'm going back to being God, because He chose to give up that privilege. It is exciting to see that the way He walked in the earth, as a man filled with the power of the Holy Spirit, is the same way we can walk. Jesus didn't come as an example FOR us. He came to be an example OF us. "In this [union and fellowship with Him], love is completed and perfected with us, so that we may have confidence in the Day of Judgment [with assurance and boldness to face Him]; because as He is, so are we in this world." (1 John 4:17) As He is, SO ARE WE in THIS WORLD. I love the clarification that we are like Him in this world and not put off until heaven. We do not evolve into being a son of God. Once we are born again we are as much a child of God as we will ever be. If we want to follow in Jesus' footsteps, it will require that we share His servant mindset. We too are called to lay down our lives for others. Will you accept the offer to be great in the kingdom? In the kingdom the way up - is first down.

Too often we separate Christianity from other parts of our life. We save things like marriage, family and vocation to manage ourselves. We punch the spiritual time clock on Sunday and put in our time for God, and without thinking about it, we claim the rest of the week for ourselves. Accepting the mindset of a servant will change your life view from merely giving God one day a week to laying your life down daily for Him as you serve others. We are called to live a life of servant hood. Serving others should be evident in our lives at home, the church and in the marketplace. Romans 12:1, in the Message Bible says, "So here's what I want you to do, God helping you: Take your everyday, ordinary life – your sleeping, eating, going to work, and walking around life, and place it before God as an offering." Since becoming a Christian, have you placed your life before God as an offering? As a Christian, our lives are to become an offering to God. In other words, we lay down our lives for His purposes. There are no higher purposes than living the life God prepared for us. We are no longer living for ourselves. As a matter of fact, the Bible says once we become a child of God we no longer belong to ourselves but now we belong to God. First Corinthians 16:19-20 says, "Do you not know that your body is the temple (the very sanctuary) of the Holy Spirit Who lives within you, Whom you have received [as a Gift] from God? You are not your own. You were bought with a price [purchased with a preciousness and paid for, made His own]. So then, honor God and bring glory to Him in your body." In the Christian vernacular, we religiously use the terms redeemed and ransomed, but do we really know what these terms mean? Ransomed means purchased out of bondage or harm. For example if someone kidnapped a person and requested a ransom, the ransom would be payment to buy back the kidnapped person. You and I were destined only for a life of sin and slavery under the grips of the devil. However, the good news of the gospel is that Jesus ransomed us. By the ransom of His blood, He purchased us which indicates He now has ownership of us. What if, as His property we lived a life dedicated daily to serving just as Jesus did? What if we put aside all that we want to help others accomplish what they want?

One of the keys to reaching the lost and the hurting is to choose a mindset of serving others. I love the way serving is described in the Message Bible in Romans 12:9-10. "Love from the center of who you are; don't fake it. Run for dear life from evil; hold on for dear life to good. Be good friends who love deeply; practice playing second fiddle." I've never played an instrument, but I remember in high school some who played in the band were given the title of "first chair trumpet" or "second chair trumpet." This designation indicated a ranking of talent and the one most proficient with their instrument was given the position of "first chair." No one ever desired to be "second chair," but all sights were set on becoming the coveted "first chair." The scripture in Romans 12 instructs us, as Christians, to do the opposite. We are to practice playing second fiddle. What does that mean? It means by practicing we can become proficient at letting others get the best spot. Now wait a minute, you might say. A few chapters earlier you were saying God wants to lift us to a place of influence. Yes, He does want to raise us up but He wants to put us there. We are to occupy ourselves with serving others and leave our promotion to Him. Philippians 2:1 in the Message Bible says, "If you've gotten anything at all our of following Christ, if his love has made any difference in your life, if being in a community of the Spirit means anything to you, if you have a heart, if you care – then do me a favor: Agree with each other, love each other, be deep-spirited friends. Don't push your way to the front; don't sweet-talk your way to the top. Put yourself aside, and help others get ahead. Don't be obsessed with getting your own advantage. Forget yourselves long enough to lend a helping hand." In order to build relationships out in the marketplace where you may have an opportunity to share the gospel with the lost, are you willing to forget yourself long enough to lend a helping hand?

Servanthood is required when seeking the lost and the hurting. When Moses questioned God about his lack of qualifications for leading the children of Israel out of Egyptian bondage, God simply responded, "What do you have in your hand?" You always have something in your hand to use – servanthood. Serving requires no prior training, experience, or references but only a willing heart that desires to see others lifted up. Opportunities mentioned in later chapters are the open doors to your city, and they are open to those who embrace servanthood. No wonder Jesus said serving was the greatest ministry in the kingdom. Serving will take you places. Do you want to reach those who are hurting? Are you willing to serve God by serving them? Serving others is a bridge that requires crossing in order to reach them.

In the gospels, Jesus used an analogy for people by classifying their role in the kingdom of God as that of being either sheep or goats. Of all the tests He could have used to separate the spiritual sheep from the goats in eternity He choose serving. "Did you feed the hungry, give the thirsty a drink, give the homeless a room, provide clothes to the naked, lay hands on the sick, and visit the sick and those in prison?" He told the disciples whenever they did these things they were doing them as unto Him. Immediately, they replied that surely they would have done these things if they saw He had these needs, but they had never seen a time when He did. This particular account is where Jesus clarifies that the heart of a servant is what is needed to possess "sheep status" in the kingdom. This is the litmus test, and the wonder of it is that it's a test anyone can pass. As you prepare to walk through the open doors of your city, will you embrace servanthood? Like Moses, what you need is already in your hand and that's all God needs to make a significant impact in the lives of others. Remember, your life is not your own. You have been purchased by God and He wants to serve through you. You belong to Him, and serving others is an essential key to building relationships in the marketplace.

THE HARVEST IS IN THE MARKETPLACE

"Jesus said to them, "Come with me. I'll make a new kind of fisherman out of you. I'll show you how to catch men and women instead of perch and bass."

Jesus (Matthew 4:19 Message Bible)

Many years ago, I heard a minister tell a story about a man who called himself a fisherman but he never went fishing. The tale went on to explain that this fisherman had spent most of his childhood around others who claimed to be fishermen, however, he'd never seen any of them with a fishing pole. He traveled to fishing conferences where he learned about bait, fishing equipment and fishing boats, yet he never fished. He read books on recognizing various kinds of fish and even attended a fishing college as a young man, but still he never fished. After he graduated, he faithfully went week after week to the river banks and discussed fishing with others who called themselves fishermen, yet none of them ever fished either. The story ended with a question, "Are you really a fisherman if you never fish?" It was obvious to me this story is comparing Christians to fishermen since Jesus told His disciples He would make them, "…fishers of men." (Matthew 4:19) Our entire experience as Christians is not to be spent learning about winning the lost, but rather we are to become involved with the lost. The number of Christians who profess to have never led one person to Jesus Christ is surprising. The mission that Jesus gave the Church as He ascended into heaven was, "Go out and train everyone you meet, far and near, in this way of life, marking them by baptism in the threefold name: Father, Son, and Holy Spirit. Then instruct them in the practice of all I have commanded you. I'll be with you as you do this, day after day after day, right up to the end of the age." (Matthew 28:18-20 Message Bible) We need to embrace the words of Jesus for reaching the lost. His instructions were to - "Go out!"

Second Corinthians 5:17-20 says, "Therefore if any person is [ingrafted] in Christ (the Messiah) he is a new creation (a new creature altogether); the old [previous moral and spiritual condition] has passed away. Behold the fresh and new has come! But all things are from God, Who through Jesus Christ reconciled us to Himself [received us into favor, brought us into harmony with Himself] and gave to us the ministry of reconciliation [that by word and deed we might aim to bring others into harmony with Him.] It was God [personally present] in Christ, reconciling and restoring the world to favor with Himself, not counting up and holding against [men] their trespasses [but canceling them], and committing to us the message of reconciliation (of the restoration to favor). So we are Christ's ambassadors, God making His appeal as it were through us. We [as Christ's personal representatives] beg you for His sake to lay hold of the divine favor [now offered you] and be reconciled to God." This passage enlightens us how once in Christ, we become brand new. God sees us without a past. We should see ourselves that way too. He didn't recondition us like an old piece of furniture. When we accepted Jesus as our Lord, we become a new creature in Christ. Along with becoming new, we also are made Christ's ambassadors – God's representatives – and were given the word of reconciliation to share with others. As ambassadors, our acts of kindness towards the people of our city are vital. How do you think they will know God loves them if we do not show them? We are God's hands and feet.

Our acts of kindness, as representatives, will show the hurting that we care, and as a result, they will know He cares.

There are many people living in your community who know very little about God. Our personal stories of experiencing God's goodness are intended to be shared with others. It is imperative that we reach the lost with the message that God is not mad at them. Out of our gratitude to God for rescuing us, our desire should be that others know about the favor we have been shown by God, and share with them the good news – He is not holding our sins against us! He loves us, and not only does He loves us, He likes us too! For too many years, we have relied on the professional clergy to do the praying, hospital visitation, and make all the efforts at affecting the community. Instead, the Word of God says this responsibility is to be shared by everyone who is a new creature – an ambassador – a representative. It is not noted anywhere in the scriptures, that these ministry roles are for clergy alone.

I don't believe we could ever really grasp the severity of spending all of eternity separated from God. It's only during this lifetime that a person can make Jesus the Lord of their life. Though we don't fully understand, it still should drive our actions where evangelism is concerned. Once this life is over, it's too late to make that decision. We all must share in reaping the harvest because we all are called as ambassadors of heaven. I'd like you to ask you a question. When it comes to winning the lost, where do you think the most fish can be found? Are they inside your church or inside your city? Of course there are those in your church who possibly don't know Jesus as their Savior. There may be some who have accepted Him at some point in life, but they have allowed other things to get in the way of walking in close fellowship with Him. Church is a perfect environment to love people, see them born again, restored to fellowship, and be discipled into understanding who they are in Christ. In Ephesians 4:11-12 we are told, "And His gifts were [varied; He Himself appointed and gave men to us] some to be apostles (special messengers), some prophets (inspired preachers and expounders), some evangelists (preachers of the Gospel, traveling missionaries), some pastors (shepherds of His flock) and teachers. His intention was the perfecting and full equipping of the saints (His consecrated people), [that they should do] the work of ministering toward building up Christ's body (the church)." Here the Holy Spirit, through Paul, spells out the role of the five-fold ministry. These ministries are anointed by God to help bring about the equipping of the saints. It becomes the responsibility of the equipped saints then who are anointed to go and do the work of the ministry in the marketplace. Learning about marketplace ministry, does not diminish the measure of importance of the church in our lives. But we must understand in God's economy the church exists inside the walls of our sanctuaries and inside the marketplace. Both are vital for harvesting cities.

A vast majority of people in our cities are not coming to our church or any other church for that matter. Several years ago, I spent time researching the scriptures seeking to learn more about how and where Jesus conducted His ministry. It was surprising to learn that in the New Testament of Jesus' 132 public appearances, 122 of them were in the marketplace; of the 52 parables Jesus told, 45 had a workplace context; of the 40 miracles recorded in the book of Acts, 39 of them took place in the marketplace. Jesus spent his adult life working as a carpenter until age 30. It was then that he transitioned to ministry in the workplace. Of His recorded teachings, 54% of them included content that centered on daily life experience. The results of this study greatly impacted my thinking about where ministry is to take place.

Let's look at few places where Jesus ministered out in the marketplace. In Luke 11:37-40 we find that while Jesus was preaching, a Pharisee invited him to dinner. Before the dinner the Pharisee noticed that Jesus did not wash. As a result, Jesus used this opportunity to explain to the Pharisee that God is not focused on us having polished exteriors. Jesus pointed out to the Pharisee that God is interested in the condition of our hearts and this important truth related to the Pharisee was shared simply during a dinner conversation.

In Luke 19:1-10 we find an account of Jesus traveling to Jericho. Zacchaeus, the head tax man, and who was short in stature, had climbed up into a tree to catch a glimpse of Him coming by. When Jesus got to the tree, He looked up and said, "Zacchaeus, come down, I'm going to come to your home." Everyone who witnessed the incident grumbled as to why Jesus would spend time with this crook. The custom was for tax collectors to collect tax money due to Caesar, but then collect more for their own wages. It was common that tax collectors were overly generous when it came to paying themselves. For this reason, they were not popular with the general public. Zacchaeus, hearing their grumbling, responded to Jesus, "I will give away half my income to the poor, and anyone I have cheated, I will pay back four times the damages." Jesus answered, "Today, salvation is coming to your house because the Son of Man came to find and restore the lost!" This ministry encounter occurred when Jesus passed by Zacchaeus on His journey to Jericho. It wasn't in the temple or in a religious setting. It was just Jesus going about His daily activities out in the marketplace.

In Matthew 8:23-27 Jesus was with his disciples out at sea when a storm arose. Jesus was sound asleep in the boat. "They roused him, pleading, 'Master, save us! We're going down!' Jesus reprimanded them. 'Why are you such cowards, such faint-hearts?' Then he stood up and told the wind to be silent, the sea to quiet down: 'Silence!' The sea became smooth as glass. The men rubbed their eyes, astonished. 'What's going on here? Wind and sea come to heel at his command.'" This incident occurred while Jesus was traveling in a boat with His disciples. How spiritual is that? Powerful ministry encounters happened everywhere as part of His common everyday life. Are you starting to get the picture with Jesus and ministry? His platform for ministry was wherever He went and whatever He was doing. Is it yours?

What about ministry in the early church? Acts 18:1-3 says, "After this [Paul] departed from Athens and went to Corinth. There he met a Jew named Aquila, a native of Pontus, recently arrived from Italy with Priscilla his wife, due to the fact that Claudius had issued an edict that all the Jews were to leave Rome. And Paul went to see them, and because he was of the same occupation, he stayed with them; and they worked [together], for they were tentmakers by trade." In this instance, the Apostle Paul makes friends with a couple, Priscilla and Aquila, because they had the same occupation as tentmakers. Later in this chapter, we read where this couple traveled with Paul to Syria. Not knowing exactly how long it took to sail to Syria, I can only imagine there were many nights out under the stars, they shared good conversation centered on the revelation of redemption that Paul had been given by the Holy Spirit. As Paul and his companions left Ephesus, Priscilla and Aquila remained there. While In Ephesus, they listened to a preacher named Apollos and soon realized that his knowledge stopped with the baptism of John. I like to imagine them taking Apollos out to lunch after church and "expounding on the nature of God more definitely and accurately." Here we see a couple who spent time with Paul in the marketplace making tents now being used to encourage a minister. Marketplace ministry is not secondary to pulpit ministry. Both are very important, and both have their place. On this occasion, the pulpit minister is learning the deeper things of God from marketplace ministers.

After my study, it became clear to me that the main focus of ministry should be out in the marketplace because that is where Jesus and early Christians spent the bulk of their time living and ministering. Jesus modeled for His disciples that sharing the gospel was not a religious activity but a lifestyle. Acts 1:8 says, "But you shall receive power (ability, efficiency, and might) when the Holy Spirit has come upon you, and you shall BE My witnesses in Jerusalem and all Judea and Samaria and to the ends (the very bounds) of the earth." Notice He did not say they were to DO witnessing but rather BE witnesses. Traditionally, church members think that God has only anointed those professionals in the ministry and that most of the work happens inside the four walls of the church. Any ministry activity that does happen outside the walls of the church building, like home or hospital visitation, the congregation reasons, "we pay the profession-al clergy to do all of that." Ed Silvoso in his book, *Ekklesia* compares it to "a World Cup Soccer Championship that had gone into overtime. There are 22 players on the field in desperate need of rest, and a multitude of spectators comfortably seated in great need of exercise. Such is the picture of overworked and frustrated pastors with inactive and equally frustrated church members." We need to accept that God has anointed each one of us as marketplace ministers to bless our cit-ies outside of the church walls. Marketplace ministry is also different than conducting community outreach programs. An outreach pro-gram usually occurs at a set time for a few hours in a set location and the focus is for church members to reach out to those living in that area of town. Sometimes churches have monthly feeding programs or summer activities for kids - all which can have tremendous impact. However, marketplace ministers are those who embrace God's call-ing and the awareness that His kingdom is to be infused into any place that they go. This includes going to work, school or just out for recreation. Marketplace ministers aren't called to fulfill the same function as the fivefold ministry mentioned in Ephesians chapter 4, but their function is necessary and every bit as vital to the harvest. Think about your own life. If you go to church meetings two or three times a week, you still spend much more time at work, in your neigh-borhood, or in some other location.

Habakkuk 2:14 in the Message Bible says, "The earth fills up with the awareness of God's glory as the waters cover the sea." How do you think the earth will be covered with the awareness of God as completely as the waters cover the sea? How will God accomplish this? God intends the awareness of Himself to spread by the influ-ence of people. Think about the career you chose. God has dis-tributed so many varying talents among us, that by our jobs alone we spread ourselves throughout the earth covering the fields of edu-cation, healthcare, science, industry, construction, law enforcement, farming, fashion, or banking. The beauty of marketplace ministry is that a substantial amount of it can be accomplished as we go about our daily activities. What if every day you go to work with a mindset like the Good Samaritan and watch for God to reveal to you the "one on your path" that day who needs His love? I can promise - you will always find them. They could be working next to you, or your work might lead you to them, but they are there.

Two women in my church, who have shared a few of their experiences with me, provide clear illustrations of marketplace ministers. One has been an instructor in a nursing program at a technical college for over twenty years. The program allows students to earn their licensed practical nursing (LPN) degree in one year. Often this class is made up of single moms, single dads or those who are rebuilding their lives in some way. The program teaches students the required skills to enter a medical profession where the wages start at a higher rate than that of retail sales, the food industry or customer service. It's a sought-after program because, upon graduation, jobs are easy to find. Oftentimes my friend tells me of students who have come to her with life challenges unrelated to nursing. As she develops a rapport with the students, opportunities arise to pray for them, share the gospel, and even encourage them with the Word of God. She is a marketplace minister. What is she accomplishing as a marketplace minister? This instructor is sowing seeds of the gospel into the unsaved, showing them that God loves them. And to some who are Christians, she is discipling them. Marketplace ministry comes naturally to her. Over the years she has impacted many for the kingdom of God.

The other woman works as a pharmacist. In the pharmacy, there is a window for dropping off prescriptions and another window for pick up. She shared that almost everyone who visits the pharmacy is ill, injured, or has a family member who is sick. Oftentimes they will confide in her by sharing their concerns while she is waiting on them. Since she knows God lives within her, and realizes that her job is her ministry, she will ask people if they would like her to pray for them. Many times, they respond favorably. After prayer some have reported immediately feeling better while others return to the pharmacy a few days later to share their story of a speedy recovery, believing that her prayer was instrumental in their healing. She feels that people are so receptive to receiving healing prayer from their pharmacist, that she now envisions the pharmacy as having a third window which is one for prayer! What if this woman believed that all evangelism, outreach, and prayer for others had to take place within the four walls of her church? Do you think her impact would be as great as it is by recognizing her mission is out in the marketplace?

Through your job you are positioned out in the marketplace to make a tremendous difference. You can make a difference by trusting God's blessing upon your life to solve challenges facing your company, or those within the community, and to touch the lives of all those around you in the process. Have you ever considered your job as your ministry and your work as your worship? This does not mean that you expect your boss to pay you for eight hours to preach to your fellow employees or leave gospel literature around the workplace. I'm saddened by some who openly profess their faith on the job, but then their actions don't confirm what they speak. Remember this, out of 100 people, you might be the one who is reading your Bible, but the other 99 are reading you! Your witness to your boss should be that you are the best employee they have.

The Bible instructs us in Colossians 3:22-24, "Servants, obey in everything those who are your earthly masters, not only when their eyes are on you as pleasers of men, but in simplicity of purpose [with all your heart] because of your reverence for the Lord and as sincere expression of your devotion to Him. Whatever may be your task, work at it heartily (from the soul), as [something done] for the Lord and not for men, Knowing [with all certainty] that it is from the Lord [and not from men] that you will receive the inheritance which is your [real] reward. [The One Whom] you are actually serving [is] the Lord Christ (the Messiah)." Do you know people on the job who only work hard when the boss is looking? We all have seen that happen out in the workplace. As Christians we are called to do our work for One who is much higher than our company supervisor. We are called to work with all our heart as unto the Lord as an expression of our devotion to Him. When we are working as unto the Lord, then we can also expect to be promoted by Him. Psalm 75:6-7 says, "For not from the east nor the west nor from the south come promotion and lifting up. But God is the Judge!" In all of our work it is essential that our eyes remain on Him - and promotion will come. Your job is not your source of supply but only one resource. God is to be our Source of supply! Having this kind of mindset will help you see your work as a mission. My current job is not one I would have ever envisioned as part of my story, but I realize it is God's path for me. Every day when I go to work - it is a mission. I've come to see my city in a new way and as I have, I've embraced it in my heart. I have the opportunity to trust God for ideas and His favor to bring resources to our city to help those whose lives are broken down by calamity. In the process, I have built relationships with many wonderful folks I would not have met by just going to church. Relationships with colleagues are formed through spending time together while we work on various projects. I've already seen evidence that God is impacting some of their lives through my ministry in the marketplace. With others I continue to lift them up in prayer and reach out in genuine kindness as opportunities present themselves.

As laborers in the field we must understand that it is the role of the Holy Spirit to reveal to people that they need a Savior. In John 16, Jesus says, speaking of the Holy Spirit, that, "When He comes, He will convict and convince the world and bring a demonstration to it about sin and about righteousness (uprightness of heart and right standing with God)." Jesus said the ministry of the Holy Spirit is to convince folks of their need to make Jesus the Lord of their lives. Our job is to present Jesus to them and show them He cares about them through our caring. A principle we can learn from the Apostle Paul in 1 Corinthians 3:6 is, "I planted, Apollos watered, but God [all the while] was making it grow and [He] gave the increase." In this passage, Paul indicates that for spiritual impact and growth, multiple contacts with people are to be expected and he relates the principle to planting and watering a seed. The important thing to remember is that we can count on God to make the eternal seed of His Word grow in the lives of people whenever we plant it and water it.

Wisdom for effective marketplace ministry can be found in James 1:19. In the Message Bible it says, "Post this at all the intersections, dear friends: Lead with your ears, follow up with your tongue, and let anger straggle along in the rear." A personal goal of mine is to become a better listener. By this, I mean being a more sensitive listener to God and to others. I like how the Message Bible says, "Lead with your ears." Your own walk with God is a key to impacting your city. Jesus said of His own ministry that He said or did nothing unless He heard it from the Father first. God knows every detail about your town and all those who live in it. As you are sensitive to Him, you will find the compassion for your city growing. Ministry will flow from this compassion, and marketplace ministry becomes a genuine response. Daniel 11:32 tells us the people that know God will be strong and do exploits. Remember you will never love your city more than God does. You are the conduit for His love reaching them so listen to His Word, and listen to your heart as you go into the marketplace. The more acquainted you are with God, the more familiar you become with the ways in which He works. Then you will find yourself paying attention to things you might not have ever noticed before.

Listening is also a prominent key to reaching people. Normally you would think people would follow a leader because of hearing them speak, but scripture says to lead with your ears. Practice listening to others without trying to formulate in your mind what you will say next. When you do this, the quality of your hearing will improve. In the marketplace being a good listener is an essential ingredient to fishing. Your work will expose you to hearing about community challenges or the hardship many individuals are facing. As you listen and open up your heart, God will begin to reveal to you how valued your city and its residents are to Him. When this begins to happen, you will find yourself asking God how He can use you to bring relief of the challenges and hardship. This is intercession – approaching

God on behalf of another. Compassion opens the door for the miraculous and ushers in God's power. It will cause you to see folks the way God sees them and not just co-workers, neighbors or the masses that make up your town. Some of the slightest actions of kindness towards others will end up occupying a large place in their hearts. This is true for anyone who will open up their heart to the needs of others, and as marketplace ministers, we should excel at this.

I met a couple of tattoo artist's one summer downtown at an art festival where they were participating in an urban art contest. When an opportunity presented itself to work with students attending the local alternative high school on an art project, I remembered how talented these artists were. After contacting them, they were excited to help and I knew the teenagers would enjoy the interaction with these young men. Their tattoo shop was advertised as a "drug-free" workplace, (an important reassurance for the school) so I arranged with the school administrators for these artists to come to give a few art lessons. One day while several kids were painting portions of a thirty foot canvas mural that depicted our town's history, one of the artists was having extreme neck pain. I asked him if he knew in the Bible that Jesus healed sick people, and I told him I believed that He still was healing today. I then asked, "Would you be willing for me to pray for your neck?" He replied, "Sure, I went to church a few times as a kid so I know about prayer." After a short prayer he began moving his neck around with more freedom. The other tattoo artist was watching and remarked, "There is some crazy energy coming out of you." I knew it was really the presence of God!

As we spent time with the students, the two artists heard some of the kids say that they didn't have enough food to eat at home, and most days the only food they had to eat was what they received in school. The Christmas break was approaching. One of the artist's, who owned two tattoo shops, told me as a dad himself he couldn't stand the thought of the kids at home for two weeks without adequate food. So he came up with the idea of doing a food drive through his business. For about 6 weeks customers who came in for a tattoo had to bring in a donation of canned goods to help the students. In this short time, he collected a U-Haul sized truck full of food which he delivered to the high school. As a result, every student had a box of groceries to take home with them for the Christmas break! After we finished our art project, one of the tattoo artists moved away to another state and for months I didn't see the artist who owned the shops. One day I learned that his brother had passed away so I sent him a message expressing my condolences. A few nights later, he sent a text to my phone saying he was struggling with depression over the loss of his brother. He shared that except for the funeral he had not left his house in two weeks. Again there was another opportunity, in the marketplace to minister the love of God. I asked God to comfort his grief and told him I was lifting him up in my prayers. A week or so after this exchange, he texted me again to tell me that he was still sorrowful, but no longer overcome by depression, and he had appreciated my concern and prayers. Much like this experience, as you walk through new opportunities within in your city to serve others, you will encounter people who are unchurched and have no idea that God loves them. If you lead with your ears and listen and respond from your heart, God will show them how much He cares about them by your caring for them. Never forget that you are an ambassador of heaven sent to bring God's kingdom to earth.

I would encourage you to visit the website of Dr. Ed Silvoso's ministry, Transform Our World. (https://transformourworld.org/) I have learned valuable principles from his ministry regarding city transformation and his international transformation team. In 2015 I enrolled in a ten-week online course titled The School of Transformation. (https://transformourworld.org/transformationondemand/university/classes/)

Dr. Silvoso is a recognized leader for his teaching role in the movement of city transformation. For decades, he and his wife served as pastors in Argentina facing community-wide hardships caused by violent drug cartels. There he lived out the principles he presents now. On the website you can listen to inspiring testimonies of anointed marketplace ministers from around the world from many professional backgrounds. As you watch or read these stories, open up your heart to God and the possibility that He wants to use you in a similar way to transform your city.

JESUS' MODEL FOR REACHING YOUR CITY

"Go then and make disciples of all the nations,
baptizing them into the name of the Father
and of the Son and of the Holy Spirit."

Jesus(Matthew 28:19)

There are three places in the gospels where Jesus commissions His followers out into ministry. In Luke chapter 9 He sends His twelve disciples, in Luke 10 seventy more and in Matthew 28 and Mark 16 He commissions all those who would ever believe on Him. In each case his instructions for ministry are very similar for each group. Let us take a look at the passage in Luke 10:1-11 where we observe the model He gave the seventy for reaching their city. For years I wondered why Jesus said that the harvest is abundant and the laborers are few, but of the two groups, it was the laborers He instructed us to pray for. To me it seemed we should pray for the harvest since they are the ones without Christ. Growing up, farming was not a part of my childhood. I cannot remember a time when my parents ever planted a vegetable garden, but only flowers were planted around the front of our house that my mother loved to tend. My husband Jonathan had been raised around gardens all of his life and for many years when we visited his parents in Arkansas they still lived on a small farm. Since we've been married, Jonathan has at times planted tomato plants and a few fruit trees, but over the past ten years his favorite growing project are his prized blackberries. One thing I've learned about harvest by watching him grow blackberries, is that around mid-July he will begin checking the bushes once or twice a week for ripened berries. Fruit that he finds ripened; he picks, washes thoroughly, and then will put them in the freezer. By the time August rolls around the harvest action quickens and he now checks the bushes every night bringing in more and more berries. From this, I learned that the closer it is to the end of harvest season, the more work there is to be done.   At the end of the harvest he gathers in more berries in a night than he had gathered in a whole week back in July. He knows if he doesn't get the berries harvested at the appropriate time, there will come a time when he can harvest no more because the berries will have spoiled. I learned from watching my husband harvest blackberries, why Jesus said to pray for the laborers instead of for the harvest.

Since God identifies lost mankind as the precious fruit of the earth that must be harvested, it's important to understand that the same principles of harvest apply to God's precious fruit as well as Jonathan's blackberries. The principled learned is this, the later it is in the season, the greater the volume of fruit that must be harvested. In Matthew 20 Jesus illustrates this truth with the parable of a vineyard owner. The owner of the estate goes out in the morning to hire the first workers and explains to them the amount of wages he will pay for their laboring in the vineyard all day long. The owner goes back at noon and then in the afternoon to hire more workers. At the end of the day, he goes back one final time to hire more. Closer to the end of the day, the last workers hired will only have a short time left to work. When the day ends the owner goes to pay all the workers.   Those who were hired first were paid the agreed amount but they notice that those who worked only the last hour were paid the same amount - so they started to complain. I don't believe Jesus is giving a lesson about fair wages in this parable. Instead, I believe He is illustrating the fact that the workers who went to work at the end of the day had much more fruit to gather in because that's the way the harvest works. Because these laborers gathered so much more fruit they were paid the same amount as those who worked all day long.

With a world population exceeding seven billion people, we now have the largest harvest to be gathered that has ever been known to mankind. According to the principles of harvest, more fruit is to be gathered in a short period of time near the end of the season, then all the other previous harvest periods combined. God desires to reap the most precious fruit of the earth, but He needs our help. If laborers are unwilling to work in the harvest or others are disinterested, God still only has one plan to bring in the harvest - through the laborers. I can see why this landowner went back out multiple times during the day to continue hiring workers because the end of the harvest season yields the largest amount of fruit. We are living in a time when the Greatest Farmer of all is seeking to reap the largest crop of all!

When Jesus commissioned the seventy, He gave them four steps to follow as they went out into their city. It is important we follow in the same order in which He instructed them. First He tells them to speak peace and blessing on every house they come to. One of the most powerful prayers we can pray for the lost (or anyone) is to bless them. A few chapters back I shared about the importance of The Blessing in our lives. God speaking Blessing over us was completely unmerited on our part. He put The Blessing in motion for our lives long before we knew about it and we certainly did nothing to deserve it. This is called God's "grace." Grace is the mystery that the devil did not understand. As long as man has existed it has been reasonable to expect that if someone acted kindly towards another, there should be reciprocation. We know this is not always the case, but often it is. But someone to act kindly towards an enemy is not natural. When we bless those we work with or our neighbors, we are acting like God. They've done nothing to earn this blessing, but yet we are speaking it over them. I like to think of our blessing others like a laser. A laser is a concentration of light that when pointed at one object can be a powerful force. A laser can effectively be used by a surgeon to remove a cataract from someone's eye or cut something as hard as a piece of steel. We can be that kind of targeted light, God's light, in the life of others.

Over the years I have often been asked by people how they can know what God's calling and plan is for their life. In 1 Peter 3:9 it says, "Never return evil for evil or insult for insult (scolding, tongue-lashing, berating), but on the contrary blessing [praying for their welfare, happiness and protection, and truly pitying and loving them]. For know that to THIS YOU HAVE BEEN CALLED, that you may inherit a blessing [from God-that you may obtain a blessing as heirs, bringing welfare and happiness and protection]." In this verse we are told that we are called to bless others. Of all the ways God may use our lives differently, blessing others is something we are all called to do. James 3:9-10 speaks of the tongue and says, "With it we bless the Lord and Father, and with it we curse men who were made in God's likeness! Out of the same mouth come forth blessing and cursing. These things, my brethren, ought not to be so." When we criticize or complain about our neighbors, family or city, we are actually speaking a curse over the people involved. As my eyes were opened to this truth it radically changed my thinking when it came to talking about others. Most the time when we are upset with someone, this person is not a stranger to us. Often, it can even be the people we love the most. However, when we get upset, we are still called to bless them in prayer instead of criticizing or telling others what they have done to us. This is where the real power lies to change a situation, but if we give in to speaking negatively then there is no power for change. That is why Jesus said when you go out into your town start by speaking a blessing. We need to pray a blessing over our neighborhood, our workplace and our city. Pray a blessing over the individuals dwelling or working in each location. As you pray and speak a blessing, think of it as using God's laser and a powerful force focused on the intent to bring change. If you disagree with the direction of your city government, rather than complain to all you meet, what if you started speaking a blessing over the city leaders? God might lead you to take other actions, but start by speaking blessing. When you are complaining, the scriptures say it is the same as if you are speaking a curse over them.

The next step Jesus gave the seventy was if people welcomed you in, then go in and fellowship with them. Too many times Christians become isolated behind the walls of their church when Jesus' model of ministry includes fellowshipping with those we meet out in the marketplace. This is a powerful method Jesus gives. He said if you are not welcomed, to brush the dust off your feet and keep moving on to the next location. To me, this is saying, there is much work to be done so don't be slowed down by those not opened to receive you yet. Once you begin to bless your neighborhood and workplace, watch and see where you begin to become "welcome." I always consider being welcomed as an indication of God at work in the person who is welcoming me into their life in some way, even if just in a small way at first. Often at work there can be activities around lunches or meetings over coffee that will provide an avenue for fellowship.

Fellowship is the prelude to building a genuine relationship with anyone. Jesus said when you are welcomed in, fellowship and don't avoid them. We all have many things in common from our daily family situations to stress on the job, and we all are faced with challenges whether as a believer or non-believer. During our fellowship there can be opportunities to share how you might be handling a situation as a believer that might be very similar to something they are facing. All the while you are sowing eternal seeds of hope into their hearts. Remember in the previous chapter we learned that some will plant and others will water, but God will give the increase. I have had community meetings end and someone will linger behind to talk to me. The next thing I know they are opening up to me about hardships they are facing. If they have "welcomed" me into their life and through fellowship I have developed a relationship with them, I will ask if I can pray for them or at times even with them. On several occasions while praying with someone, I've sensed God's presence fill the Board Room or my office. I always feel as though He is smiling and appreciates me for taking Him into the marketplace to love those whom I meet there. There have been times people start weeping under the presence of God's goodness. What is happening at times like this? I am filling the earth with the awareness of Him – in the marketplace!

The third step of Jesus' commission to the seventy was that after they fellowshipped with those who welcomed them, they were to heal the sick in the house. In other words they were to meet a felt need. We live in a time when the world desperately needs to see the power of God. The gospel was never meant to be preached only, but was to be demonstrated also. We should develop expectancy that signs and wonders accompany us out in the marketplace. Jesus said they would and He has never changed His mind about it. A woman with whom I worked very closely with on a project told me she was struggling with health problems which resulted in not being able to see out of one of her eyes. I asked if it would make her uncomfortable if I prayed for her, and she favorably responded. While praying, her sight was improved in that eye, and she began to cry. We both could sense an overwhelming awareness of God's presence filling the room. This resulted in many other opportunities to share the gospel with her and to enjoy genuine friendship and fellowship around growing spiritually.

Physical healing is part and parcel of the gospel of Jesus Christ. First John chapter 3 verse 8 says that the purpose for which Jesus came was to undo the works of the devil. Since Jesus spent two-thirds of His earthly ministry healing those who were physically sick, He made it clear that sickness is a work of the devil that He came to undo. Then the early church followed His example. They regularly saw healing miracles take place as was recorded in the Book of Acts. Signs and wonders have never been removed from our commissioning because we serve the God of miracles! How much more do we need the miraculous today to prove to the lost that God is alive and loves them? I'm not at all opposed to the medical system and have relied on it for myself and my family many times. Several of my close friends and colleagues are dedicated to the medical profession. Doctors are at times more receptive to believing God is the Healer than some preachers are. Some have shared that they realize medical training adds a part to the process, but they know overall the healing comes from God. However, you can't go one day without the news reporting problems within healthcare systems. The rising cost of healthcare, people being denied healthcare, and people experiencing problems when using the healthcare system cause many to agree we are facing healthcare challenges both on national and global levels.

If you attend a church that observes the ordinance of communion I have some good news for you. In 1 Corinthians 11:23-26, the Apostle Paul said that he received instructions from the Lord Himself on administering communion. This ordinance first enacted by Jesus with His disciples before His betrayal and then now through Paul teaching the early church included using two elements - both the bread and drink. Paul said we are to practice this method of communion by using two elements until the Lord comes again. I believe this is saying that the shelf-life expiration date on communion will be the date Jesus returns. Therefore until that time communion consists of remembering His shed blood AND His broken body. According to Isaiah 53:4-5 which says, "Surely He has borne OUR grief's (sicknesses, weaknesses, and distresses) and carried OUR sorrows and pains [of punishment], yet we [ignorantly] considered Him stricken, smitten and afflicted by God [as if with leprosy]. But He was wounded for OUR transgressions, He was bruised for OUR guilt and iniquities; the chastisement [needful to obtain] peace and well-being for US was upon Him and with the stripes [that wounded] Him WE are healed and made whole." His shed blood was representative of the remission of our sins and His broken body was symbolical for the physical healing of our bodies. Why then should we live as if only the blood is still working? Many who attend church regularly are certain that the blood continues to effectively cleanse us of our sins, but then so many of these same people lack a confidence in the work of His broken body. Was Jesus a more effective sin bearer than He was as a sickness bearer? Of course not! It's just that we've believed more in the work of His blood because that's all many have been taught in church. Let us go into the marketplace where we are welcomed and trust God to answer our prayers for those we meet who are in need of physical healing. If this was an impossible undertaking, then Jesus would not have included it in His commission to the seventy and to us in Mark 16:18 where He says we are to "lay hands on the sick and they will get well." If Jesus has ascended into heaven (which He physically has) and we are called the Body of Christ (which we are) then it's our hands in the earth that Jesus will use in order for Him to heal the sick. Healing comes from Him, but He works through our hands and our obedience. Sickness and disease are still a work of the devil that Jesus came to undo and He is the same yesterday, today and forever!

This city-reaching step instructs us that we need to expect to meet a felt need in the lives of those we encounter out in the marketplace. I want to emphasize the significance of following the steps in the order that Jesus laid them out in His city reaching model. By meeting a felt need in someone's life we can demonstrate that we care about them. But this opportunity might not present itself without first spending time in fellowship with them. You may encounter someone who is suffering from depression and despair - you can bring encouragement and hope. Perhaps it could be something as simple as providing a winter coat to a person who doesn't have one. What if you met a need like volunteering to teach literacy skills in your local library? Not only would you meet the need of teaching people to read but this outreach could possibly lead to them finding a higher paying job. By teaching them to read you might help to improve their financial status as well. The significance of meeting a felt need is this - people who don't know God do not understand that their greatest need in life is actually a spiritual need. Too many times as Christians we feel we must first discuss spiritual matters when fellowshipping with non-believers when the non-believers are not yet asking those kinds of questions. Jesus said to start first by meeting a natural need they have - then preach the gospel.

I have learned so much through this city-reaching step of Jesus' model. Not only do individuals have needs, but cities have needs as well. When you believe God to meet a felt need in your community through you, He will raise you to a new place of influence in your city. Trust me when I say that your city has needs. Some of them are staggering. In my region, we lead the nation in having the highest numbers of babies being born to drug addicted mothers. Then the baby is born with an addiction. Leaders in my state say that we could lose a whole generation to opioid addiction. The average statistic for most cities for babies born to an addicted mother is six out of every one thousand births but in my community it is fifty-eight out of every one thousand who are born addicted. Daily in my town, the emergency dispatch system answers an average of nine calls related to domestic violence. Children are going to school on a regular basis after witnessing acts of violence in their home. Have you ever considered being a catalyst to meeting a felt need like these within in your city? I heard recently that there are over twelve thousand churches in operation in my state. If this is true, then why do we have the kinds of challenges we are facing? Twelve-thousand churches, filled with believers who sincerely love God, and yet still all around us we see an epidemic of addiction and violence. Could it be that we have never even considered God would meet these needs through believers? What if believers who are attending local churches on Sunday take the power of God out into the marketplace on Monday? Could it be that the clergy in these thousands of churches are void of an understanding of what marketplace ministry is and therefore, they are not equipping their congregations for such tasks?

Romans 5:20 says, "But where sin increased and abounded, grace (God's unmerited favor) has surpassed it and increased the more and superabounded." These challenges I've listed facing my city and other cities as well, clearly indicate that sin is abounding. But where is the superabounding? Why not believe The Blessing is upon us as marketplace ministers? In partnership with our local churches, we could rid our towns of the epidemic of drugs and crime. Then superabounding would be evident! I love Ephesians 1:20 in the Message Bible which says, "All this energy issues from Christ: God raised him from death and set him on a throne in deep heaven, in charge of running the universe, everything from galaxies to governments, no name and no power exempt from his rule. And not just for the time being, but forever. He is in charge of it all, has the final word on everything. At the center of all this, Christ rules the church. THE CHURCH YOU SEE, IS NOT PERIPHERAL TO THE WORLD; THE WORLD IS PERIPHERAL TO THE CHURCH. The church is Christ's body, in which he speaks and acts by which he fills everything with his presence." The real is news is not what is going on in the world but what is going on in the church. The local or national news reporters may not report it on the news that way but that's the way God views it and so should we.

Do you think it is the will of God that families be torn apart by a loved one's drug addiction or witness them living a lifestyle of crime? This is clearly the work of the thief that Jesus said comes to steal, kill and destroy (John 10:10). When police officers take their oath, it's not left up to their interpretation whether or not they think it is a good idea to "protect and to serve" because that is the nature of their commissioning. In the same way, let us accept the commission of Luke 10 and expect to meet the felt needs in every town where we have a welcome platform for marketplace ministry. Let us resist the devil and stand up in the power of the Holy Spirit. We should refuse to allow our city to be overtaken by evil and expect felt-needs to be met by the superabounding grace of God. What if you took a little time to do some research to find out what the greatest needs are that your city is facing? You might already be aware of what they are. Then begin to bless your city in prayer. As you bless in prayer, God will direct your steps toward places and the people with whom you can build relationships and begin meeting felt needs. Maybe He will lead you to mentor at-risk children, begin a job-skill training program, or to launch a food-box outreach. Whatever steps you take, don't focus on the steps. Envision these steps as the bridge you cross to walk through open doors to those you would never meet just by attending church every Sunday. This will bring you into the heart of your city where God wants His grace to superabound. Second Chronicles 16:9 says, "For the eyes of the Lord run to and fro throughout the whole earth to show Himself strong in behalf of those whose hearts are blameless towards Him." This tells us God is looking for places to show Himself strong. Get involved in the city in the midst of the greatest areas of challenge! Let us lift our voices in prayer and tell God we have found just the kind of place He's been looking for. He is welcome to show Himself strong here in our city!

The last step Jesus gave in His commission to the seventy was that after they had blessed the city in prayer, fellowshipped wherever they were welcomed, brought healing to the hurting, - then they were to tell them the "kingdom of God has come near to you." (Luke 10:9) As you proclaim the gospel you are giving them the opportunity to step over into the Kingdom of God! Romans 1:16 says, "For I am not ashamed of the Gospel (good news) of Christ, for it is God's power unto salvation [for deliverance from eternal death] to everyone who believes with a personal trust and a confident surrender and firm reliance, to the Jew first and also to the Greek." In this final step we reach the pinnacle of where the other three steps were leading. The gospel is the power of God, and as we share it in the marketplace we scatter eternal seeds that God will cause to grow. Even if it appears not well received, you still have sown it. Several times throughout the Book of Acts the Apostle Paul shares his story of conversion to Christianity. He tells of hearing Stephen preach the gospel before Stephen is stoned to death for his faith. Paul (Saul at the time) stood there and held the coat of Stephen. No one would have guessed while witnessing this horrific act that Stephen's words impacted Paul in any way but Paul said they did. Why? They did because the gospel contains the power of God. Have faith when you share seeds of the gospel that God will make them grow.

In the Book of Acts chapter 10 we find the story of a Roman officer named Cornelius. Scripture says he feared God, gave generously to the poor, and was a man of prayer. God responded to his prayers and sent an angel who told him where to find a man named Simon Peter who would preach the gospel to him. Cornelius sent for Peter and four days later Peter arrived and preached the gospel to Cornelius and his family who were all gathered together in the house. The Bible says that the Holy Spirit fell upon them all and they were filled with the Holy Spirit and then Peter baptized them in water. This passage is insightful because Cornelius was not of the Christian faith, yet he feared God, prayed, and he was a generous giver. Whatever religion he was so devoutly practicing, God responded to him by providing the means for him and his household to be born again. Notice also when the angel appeared to him, he told him to send for Peter (a man) who would preach the gospel to them in order to be saved. This illustrates that God hasn't ordained angels to preach the gospel but people. We as His representatives are those who hold the glorious message of reconciliation.

As ambassadors of heaven, we are to tell folks that God is not mad at them and wants them to be reconciled to Him. Romans 5:9 says, "Therefore, since we are now justified (acquitted, made righteous, and brought into right relationship with God) by Christ's blood, how much more [certain is it that] we shall be saved by Him from the indignation and wrath of God." Jesus saved us from the wrath of God and through His death on the cross and resurrection, He has now has reconciled us to God. All that is left is for us to accept this free gift of salvation. The only sin that will send someone into a Christ-less eternity is the sin of rejecting Jesus. In this final step we are to share the gospel, and the Holy Spirit will do the convincing. What a blessed partnership we are called into with God. Jesus is the Head, and we are the Body. The Head is in heaven while we are in the ones in the earth. But it is all one work and the city-reaching model Jesus commissioned. Throughout my lifetime, with great awe, I've beheld several magnificent wonders of nature like the roaring

Niagara Falls, the Rocky Mountains covered with snow and the mountains of Appalachia filled with a brilliance of red, yellow and orange fall colors. But do you know what a breathtaking sight to God is? "To Him it is the sight of feet going out to preach the gospel! "And how can men [be expected to] preach unless they are sent? As it is written, How beautiful are the feet of those who bring glad tidings! [How welcoming is the coming of those who preach the good news of His good things!]" (Romans 10:15)

TREAT YOUR CITY WITH KINDNESS

"You keep track of all my sorrows. You have collected all my tears in your bottle. You have recorded each one in your book."

(Psalm 56:8 New Living Translation)

In 2012, when I was hired by the police department as the director of a large crime-reduction grant, the overall goal of the project was to reduce drug-related and violent crime in two neighborhoods historically known for the highest rates of these crimes. As I have mentioned earlier, this project required a collaborative problem-solving approach where I engaged community partners to assist in recognizing the causal factors of crime. Together, we implemented evidence-based practices for crime reduction. With God's favor, the program quickly accelerated. Within the first year, we had 33 agencies implementing 19 programs that addressed crime prevention, neighborhood revitalization, increased policing, and offender treatment, all with the goal of crime reduction. As mentioned in the introduction, in 2014, our project received national recognition by winning a prestigious criminal justice award and was listed by the U.S. Department of Justice as a "Success Story." The goal of the offender-intervention program was for the purpose of reducing recidivism. The program accepted referrals made through the criminal court. The two qualifiers were that the person had felony charges and addictions. This population had considerable risks for committing new crimes or violating probation, and potentially returning to jail within one to three years after previously being incarcerated. For the nearly four years, I oversaw the development of this program; I learned a great deal by first-hand involvement with many of the offenders. During this time, I became aware of the prevalence of trauma that most of these individuals had experienced in their lives. A vast majority of those with a criminal history suffer from addictions as well. What really captured my attention was how many in this cycle of incarceration or addictions have a common childhood history of being abused, neglected or violently victimized. This is in no way an excuse for crime or addictions, but it opened my eyes to a possible explanation for them.

Our city and county experience a high rate of domestic violence evidenced by the average of nine calls per day mentioned earlier. To those in larger cities, this may seem like a small number, but our population is just over 60,000 people. Also during the time period in which those domestic violence calls were tracked, 100% of all the homicides committed in our county were due to acts of domestic violence. Along with a domestic violence crisis, residents in our community suffer disproportionately from the effects of substance abuse and corresponding sequela such as criminal behavior, child abuse, and neglect. As mentioned earlier, in our region we unfortunately have one of the highest, if not the highest, rate of babies born addicted to opioids. Our state is second in the nation in number of opioid prescriptions per person. These health and crime issues emphasize the need for systems to collaborate in order to increase prevention and treatment efforts for citizens in our region.

My lengthy career background in crisis-intervention programs includes working in faith-based programs, and intensive outpatient drug recovery, facilitating classes for juvenile courts in two counties, and most recently working with this probation program. Often, I've heard stories I'll never forget. The majority of these stories came from teens or adults who experienced traumatic childhood events that have now become a part of their stories. Hearing these told, I found myself showing empathy to these individuals before even I realized how important empathy was to a trauma survivor in validating his/her story. To me, it seemed so unfair that someone experienced a childhood raised by a parent addicted to heroin. I cannot grasp leaving a child alone at six years old, for two weeks, along with her ten year old sister and a four week old infant sister, while their mother traveled to another state in search of drugs. What child deserves to have a mother who introduces her to addiction? Or a man who had a family member rape him on a regular basis starting at the age of 7? Or someone living in a home filled with violence where as a 10 year old, she came home from school one day having to step in front of a drunken, enraged father pointing a loaded shotgun at her mother? I've heard one person tell how his mother supported them by prostitution. When he was only four years old he remembered her putting him on the bed in a motel room facing the TV and turning on cartoons while she earned their living in that same bed. Several times I've responded with tears to these stories, telling the person how sorry I was for their experience - that no child should have suffered abuse like that from a parent. Sadly, to each person a very abnormal situation became normal to them.

Over the years, I reasoned that no one picks the family they are born into. In reality, I could have been born into that type of family and they could have been born into mine. As a Christian, I knew though none of us can pick where we start out in life, but with God, we don't have to let our past define our future. All of us, at times experience difficult situations that are beyond our control; many occur during our childhood. Yet with the love and support of a nurturing parent, grandparent, teacher or youth worker, we rebound in a way that the stressful situation causes us to be more resilient. But what about all these I heard from that lacked any kind of support and turned to risky behaviors to cope instead?

In 2014, the Chief of our police department tasked me with applying for grant funding to establish a Family Justice Center. A Family Justice Center is a program that co-locates all the services a victim of domestic or sexual violence requires in order to navigate this most difficult place in life. Services like legal aid, law enforcement, counseling, child protective services and even spiritual help would be available all in one location. In the course of writing the grant I visited a Family Justice Center in a nearby city. This visit was when I first encountered education related to Trauma Informed Care and Adverse Childhood Experiences (ACEs) science (https://www.samhsa.gov/capt/practicing-effective-prevention/prevention-behavioral-health/adverse-childhood-experiences). This type of education explains the negative effects that traumatic experiences can have on brain development throughout all our life. However, the greatest damage occurs when these events occur during early childhood. Simply put, it is critical to strong brain development that young children have at least one nurturing caregiver in their lives. Our early childhood experiences affect the development of brain architecture which then provides the foundation for all future learning, behavior and our health. Our brains have designated areas for learning, reasoning and regulating emotion but there is a particular part that is activated when we feel we are in danger. If this system is activated too often, development of other parts of the brain suffers. Key to a child developing healthy brain architecture is what is described as "serve and return interaction." Think of it like a tennis match - a parent serves the ball over the net, and the child returns it. Or the child hits the ball over the net to the parent, and the parent returns it. This same principle is working when a parent reads a book, repeats a word or number, or provides calming for the child when they are hurt, and the child responds. Likewise the child makes sounds or facial expressions and expects the parent to respond. However, if a child is exposed to an environment where there is chronic instability and constant danger void of a nurturing adult, they do not receive the serve and return interaction and only develop the part of the brain that is set to react to danger. This part of the brain can only respond in three ways, fight, flight or freeze. The brain areas involved in learning and self-control remain underdeveloped. So with communities battling a drug epidemic and frequent cases of domestic violence many children are being set up to fail.

From the moment I heard this, I felt the Lord impressing me to pay attention. It seemed like I was learning education about a cure of kindness and compassion that I knew my community needed. A short time later, I attended a Family Justice Center Conference in San Diego, California where I heard one of the co-investigators of the Adverse Childhood Experiences (ACE) study speak about his landmark research and experiences in this field. This physician explained the ten question ACE survey on which one point is given for each of five questions asking, "Did you see this in your home before the age of 18" and then five questions asking "Did this happen to you before you were 18?" Questions included inquiries such as, "Before your 18th birthday, did a parent or other adult in your household often or very often swear at you, insult you, put you down or humiliate you or act in a way that made you afraid that they might physically hurt you? Did you often or very often feel that no one in your family loved you or thought you were important or special or your family didn't look out for each other, feel close or support each other? Did you often feel you didn't have enough to eat, had to wear dirty clothes and had no one to protect you, or were your parents too drunk or too high to take care of you like taking you to the doctor if you needed to go? Did you ever see your mother or stepmother pushed, grabbed, slapped or had something thrown at her or was she ever threatened with a gun or knife? Did you live with anyone who was a problem drinker or alcoholic or was anyone depressed, mentally ill or has attempted suicide?"

What resonated in my thinking was how twenty years of science now validated the importance of having nurturing caregivers during childhood development are. The speaker also shared conclusive research results on the effects on the brain of a child growing up in the midst of ongoing stress. Coming from a community where opioid addiction is a major concern, it was astounding to hear that a male with an ACE score of 6 (answered yes to 6 of the 10 ACE questions) was 4,600% more likely to become an IV drug user than someone with an ACE score of 0. Just to frame the significance of this information, by comparison the American Heart Association has gone to great lengths and expense to educating the public that a lack of exercise increases the chance of a heart attack by 12% and smoking increases it by 50%. But now I was hearing that to grow up in a home where you were sexually abused, witnessed violence or had a parent with addictions, the combination of these events could vastly increase your risk of becoming an IV drug. It wasn't that they might just use drugs; this compelling information now indicated they were riding a fast train towards addiction!

In the criminal justice field there is a phrase, "cradle to prison pipeline." But who enters that pipeline? I felt I had found the missing piece of this puzzle. I heard about the prevalence of traumatic events in so many who lacked having a nurturing caregiver, mentor or faith. For many people, the abuse lasted over a period of many years. They did not learn how to respond resiliently to negative events. Also I learned that science validated how ongoing traumatic events developed a part of the brain that is not made for learning but only for survival. It was becoming clear why children were set up to fail in school as they had only developed the survival part of their brain and not the complex thinking and learning part. For many years, it has been a well-established fact that if a child can learn to read, do well in school and graduate – they greatly diminish their chance of entering into a life of crime. This new information explained the struggles of children in school which often is accompanied by bad behavior. Equipped with understanding about the effects of trauma, I urgently sensed a need to train a network of professionals armed with this information. It made sense that service providers needed to realize problem behaviors might really be telling a story of what a child is encountering at home.

Often these adverse events occur where no one outside of those directly involved witness it - except for God. Many times the perpetrators threaten victims by saying, "If you tell anyone about this, I'll bring you or ones you love greater harm." The Holy Spirit reminded me of Psalm 56: 8, "You keep track of all my sorrows. You have collected all my tears in your bottle. You have recorded each one in your book." (New Living Translation) There has been a tremendous amount of silent suffering in our generation that God has known all along. I felt compelled that He wanted to use me to raise awareness to that. I thought of Isaiah's prophetic word concerning Jesus – "Behold My Servant, Whom I uphold, My elect in Whom My soul delights! I have put My Spirit upon Him; He will bring forth justice and right and reveal truth to the nations. He will not cry or shout aloud or cause His voice to be heard in the street. A bruised reed He will not break, and a dimly burning wick He will not quench; He will bring forth justice in truth." (Isaiah 42:1-3) Jesus was anointed and sent to restore those who were bruised. Instead of extinguishing their dimly lit wick He would cause it to burn bright! Again in Luke 4, as Jesus begins His earthly ministry, He announces His platform of those He is sent to reach. "The Spirit of the Lord [is] upon Me, because He has anointed Me [the Anointed One, the Messiah] to preach the good news (the Gospel) to the poor; He has sent Me to announce release to the captives and recovery of sight to the blind, to send forth as delivered those who are oppressed [who are downtrodden, bruised, crushed, and broken down by calamity], To proclaim the accepted and acceptable year of the Lord [the day when salvation and the free favors of God profusely abound]." The Amplified Bible gives an accurate description of the effects that trauma and abuse bring to someone's life, "those who are oppressed, downtrodden, bruised, crushed and broken down by calamity." If there has ever been a generation with hundreds of thousands of lives that are broken down by calamity, it is the one in which we live!

As I continued to devour all the information that the Lord was bringing across my path, I decided this must be included into our arsenal against the region's opioid epidemic and crime reduction. In the spring of 2015, I attended a corrections conference where I met the Director of the Substance Abuse Mental Health Services Administration (SAMHSA), National Center for Trauma Informed Care (NCTIC) who spoke on Trauma Informed Care. Once again, I was convinced I was hearing a message of healing that was so urgently needed in my city. Afterwards, I introduced myself to her and explained my role in the community and my desire to educate my community on this subject. She gave me her card and told me to be in touch.

Returning home, I began a period of research on Trauma Informed Care and ACEs science, what this information looked like within various systems, and what it might look like within the network of organizations that had been assembled in my crime reduction efforts. I discovered an online publication titled, "Aces Too High" (https://acestoohigh.com/), which disclosed the implementation of this knowledge into every imaginable sector of services. These concepts are just beginning to become more widely discussed across the nation. Articles published there revealed to me how a small handful of cities in the United States have each begun creating a system of care to help heal individuals derailed by experienced abuse and trauma. The beauty of this message is that healing begins just by having someone validate (believe) the report of abuse. The road did not stop here. I decided to present my findings and vision to a group of faculty members at our state university to determine if someone would partner with me in this community education endeavor. I asked a longtime friend and Christian Psychology professor if she would attend this meeting in support. A few days following my presentation, she contacted me saying that she wanted to be the one to partner with me in educating our community. She saw it as the closest thing she'd ever heard to sharing the gospel, a message of grace and kindness but without using chapters and verse of the Bible. In our first meeting together to discuss how we could educate our community, without any budget for it at all, we committed this project to God in prayer. We told God of the three chairs at the table in my friend's office, we designated the empty one for Him. This was His project. In the following 18 months, it took off supernaturally and has spread like wildfire. I've often reflected on that moment and what happens when you invite God to partner with you in bringing healing to the wounded in your community!

In August 2015, we contacted the NCTIC's Director that I had met in Florida, asking if we could talk to strategize a game plan to educate our community. She visited in October of that year to speak to 383 professionals we assembled at the university. Due to the fact we had such a large network already in place from my crime prevention program, we were able to include many sectors of our community. In January 2016, I received from SAMHSA a draft course, "Trauma Informed Approach: Key Assumptions and Principles," which we were encouraged to use in teaching professionals how to implement this newfound understanding. I'm not sure how to describe what happened over the next several months – it was amazing! In eighteen months, my friend and I trained over 1,400 professionals in disciplines such as healthcare, and human services, addiction treatment, corrections, juvenile justice, and community services in over thirty training events.

Never has anything in my career taken off with such speed as the demand for this training. In June 2016, we held our first Trauma Informed System of Care Coalition meeting. The growing Coalition meets bi-monthly at the police department and currently has 16 organizations as system partners, including representatives from the children's hospital, public schools, Boys & Girls Club, multiple departments of the university, area non-profits, and the Family Justice Center. The reason for creating a system of care is that many who are victims are served by multiple services. If a child is in a home where domestic violence occurs, that child is not likely to be taken to a counselor the next day to process this confusing event. However, by law the child does have to attend school. It made sense to have all the frontline services speaking the same language. Then problem behaviors can be recognized as possible adaptations to trauma that might really be telling a story of abuse. Over several months, we sought grants to apply for with hopes of partnering with one of our system partners to create a Trauma Informed/ACEs science pilot program in our community. In the summer of 2016, we were awarded a grant for the creation of a demonstration project by partnering with a local at-risk youth program. In this project we are implementing "calming" activities with the children instead of a more typical first recourse of using punitive responses. This project also works with the parents providing instruction on the importance of nurturing their children. As a result of this funding, we have had the opportunity to receive groundbreaking training provided by the Department of Children's Services and the Commission on Children and Youth. Recognizing the importance of ACEs science, the state's goal is now to create a culture shift where more resources are invested early on to prevent the development of diseases, health-risk behaviors, mental-health issues, and social issues down the line. This change in public investment should produce long-term improvements by building healthy, strong, future generations of citizens. Many experts agree, these efforts could slow down the "feeder system" of individuals entering the juvenile and criminal justice systems and dismantle the "cradle to prison pipeline." One organization working in partnership with the State Aces Initiative coined the metaphor, "charging stations" for messaging the concept of building resilience. This phrase is easily understood by most within our generation. With the widespread use of smart phones and tablets among both the young, and the old, it is easily understood you need a charging station to rejuvenate your device once the battery is depleted. In the same way, each one of us needs to have a support system in place, and by recognizing this; there are so many ways marketplace ministers and churches can respond as "charging stations."

As the message of trauma-informed care and the risk of ACEs have spread in the community, our training calendar filled beyond what we could handle with all our other job responsibilities. To fulfill this demand, we created a Train-the-Trainer program and have offered it twice so far, training 79 professionals to teach a composite course we assembled. Looking back, I definitely attribute having an existing network of crime prevention partnerships already developed and functioning as a group to be a contributing factor to the speed in which our region has embraced this message of healing. As more resources become available and easily accessible through SAMHSA, Aces Too High, the Children's' Traumatic Stress Network, The Department of Justice and others, I believe we will see the outcome from this message bring healing to many communities over the next 10-15 years. God is using us to raise awareness about the prevalence of abuse and neglect that has gone unaddressed for too long. We are beginning to witness this education bringing changes to our community. As examples, one of the homeless service agencies changed portions of their intake procedures and signage to be more welcoming and less shaming; three university faculty members are now incorporating Trauma Informed Care into their curriculum; an emergent care program for children created a calm and more welcoming environment in their office; nurses at the local children's hospital reported displaying more empathy to drug-addicted mothers coming in for prenatal care, realizing there is likely a history of abuse in the mother's life as well; and several local elementary schools implemented a program called "Handle With Care." (http://www. handlewithcarewv.org/) In the Handle With Care program, law enforcement officers notify school personnel if a child in the school was present during a house call regarding a domestic violence situation. They do not release any details surrounding the event, just ask the school to "handle the student with care" in the days following.

As a parent and a grandparent, I can't ignore statements like one from a state legislator saying; in our state an entire generation could be lost to the scourge of opioid abuse. I refuse to turn my head and ignore the growing number of children witnessing domestic violence in their homes without a caring adult to help them work through trauma such as this. Because of my understanding about the prevalence of trauma and adverse childhood experiences present in so many lives, I now see people, not statistics. With the message of Trauma Informed Care and by using ACEs science, we are determined to create a community of caring. This caring community is where children may spend time after school in programs where they encounter healing advocates or school teachers who understand the impact of trauma. Instead of responding punitively when a child's behavior changes, these mentors offer empathy and ask, "What's going on?" ACEs do not excuse a life of crime or drug addiction, but offers an explanation for this behavior. Maybe over time these populations might experience empathy in their programs that will bring to their lives a greater degree of healing and recovery. As Christians, we continue to do the work of Jesus by healing those whose lives are broken down by calamity. I'm including this part of my story to encourage you that your community shares this same brokenness. Educating your city, your agency, or the school your child attends is possible. Trauma informed care is a practical way to bring an infusion of kindness and empathy with less judgment and fewer punitive responses to problem behavior seen within your city without speaking Christianese. Doors will begin to open and people will seek you out to thank you for this healing message and maybe even share their stories with you. I've ended meetings related to this topic with hugs from individuals who were crying and wanting to share their story with me of unfair abuse or victimization. I keep in my desk a file called "Trauma Stories" which contains emails I receive from professionals who after attending training felt compelled to write and tell me their own story. One of my favorite stories came from a reporter who was assigned by our largest newspaper to regularly cover many of my projects. On assignment by the newspaper, he attended a trauma-informed care training we provided for the local homeless service providers in order to report on it. His article detailing this training was entitled, "Local Organizations Learn Different Way to Approach Traumatization" and the first line of the article was, "What if all along...kindness was the cure?" At the end of the training that day he mentioned how grateful he was that he could attend and learn about this subject. About a month later, one night I received an email from him with the subject line, "sorry to bother you but wanted to tell you something." This piqued my curiosity so I continued reading. He shared with me that he'd been assigned that day to cover a story of someone who was hoarding a large pile of personal items and trash in her yard, so much so that neighbors were complaining about the nuisance of rodents. When he arrived at the house to speak to the property owner, she explained to him how her mother had passed away and all the items piled up in her yard were her mother's belongings that she had to clean out of her mother's home. She said she could not bring herself yet to part with them though they had no monetary value. Then she began to tell the reporter of abuse she'd suffered as a child at the hands of her father. Her mother was somewhat of a hero figure to her. The reporter told me he remembered the training he had attended and responded to the woman he was interviewing with compassion by saying, "I'm so sorry that you had such a difficult childhood." He said the woman looked surprised by his kindness and thanked him for his remark, and they concluded the interview. He wanted to write me to say thank you for educating him about the prevalence of abuse in the lives of those we encounter daily and how often this abuse was no fault of their own. Now by simply showing empathy a measure of healing comes. As a follow up to this story, within a few days of her story being published in the paper, several neighbors came together to help her remove the items from her yard.

My email address is in the front of this book if you would like more information on how you can bring this education to your community. Within the past year, more and more cities are beginning a conversation to address this subject and now realize how addressing child neglect and abuse early on could change the community landscape over the next ten to fifteen years. This could greatly reduce the growing stream of those headed for prison or homelessness. One thing you can be certain of – those living in our cities need to be treated with kindness.

OPEN DOORS

"I have set before you a door wide open
which no one is able to shut."

(Revelation 3:8)

The next few chapters contain the content that really inspired me to write this book. By working closely with the many systems and agencies within our city, I was enlightened to how many wide-opened doors are available for impacting the lives of thousands of folks in your community. And yet, very few Christians are walking through them. As I saw this, I began to create awareness within my own city by gathering Faith-Based Leaders together on a bi-monthly basis to share information about these open doors and opportunities. As a result several churches have members stepping into greater levels of marketplace ministry. Wherever you live your city has these very same kinds of doors that are standing wide open. They might be called by a different name but nonetheless they are there and similar to what I'm going to describe. Now more than ever is the time for Christians to walk through these doors using their gifts of service and volunteerism. However, these doors not only allow you access to those who are hurting within your city; they also give you an opportunity to infuse the presence of God into these systems. Remember, Jesus came to seek and to save "that" which is lost. He wants not only to save the people who are lost but to reclaim the systems as well.

As you step out, you will find the opportunity to follow the same model for reaching your city that Jesus laid out for the seventy in Luke 10. In the marketplace is where the harvest can be found. Too many Christians have discounted their effectiveness in reaching others or that God could use them to accomplish extraordinary deeds within their town. All along God has said HE has faith in you. The scriptures say that anyone who is a new creature in Christ is also an ambassador for heaven. But our focus should not only be on influencing people for eternity. Do you know there is more information in the Bible about us bringing heaven down to earth than there is about us taking people with us to heaven? Think about the Lord's Prayer which Jesus gave in response to the disciples asking Him to teach them how to pray. He said they were to ask that "His kingdom would come and that His will would be done on EARTH as it is in heaven!" Are you ready to bring heaven to your city? Do you want God's will to be done in your city? I pray that many are inspired by this book and will take back their cities from the enemy's grip and rescue those who are living as his captives in your community. It is my prayer that as I lay out this road map, that your heart will respond by saying, "Lord, I am willing to do that." Remember He is not looking for ability; He is only looking for your availability. Everything you've read thus far should convince you that God will empower you to get the job done. His Blessing will equip you to go places and accomplish things beyond your own education and experience.

I'm going to first discuss the public systems within your city and then later the non-profits. Every city has some form of these same public systems. Along with defining the role of each, I'm going to list ways I've discovered you can get involved with them. I will do the same by describing non-profits that are found in your community and ways you can offer to serve through them.

God never ordained that our government provide the rescue our towns and citizens need but for many years we've largely left it up to the government. As a result there now are massive funding requirements for these programs and struggles to meet the growing demands for services being asked of them. Many of these systems are very welcoming of community assistance. I want to preface this by saying that it's important as you approach any system or non-profit in your community that you follow the Luke 10 pattern by blessing them in prayer first. As you begin to bless these entities in your community in prayer and then reach out to offer service, follow the leading of "welcoming." When one service turns you away, go right on to another. You will find one that will welcome your involvement, and that is where you should begin. Also, remember it's not necessary to say anything about your faith in the beginning, but explain you are offering time and service to help. Be sure to do exactly what the organization asks of you in the manner in which they ask it. Your first step in going through the open door is one of gaining trust; so doing what they ask of you is critical. Once an organization trusts you and realizes you are sincerely there to help, you begin to build relationships through fellowship. Some of you might experience an opportunity similar to Joseph in the Bible and see some aspect of a particular system turned over to you. You might not be asked to run the public schools or jail system, but once you prove you are there to help, you may be asked to serve on a board or task force to help solve the challenges faced by the system. This happens regularly to me. Remember that God will cause you to be the head and not the tail. He has provided you with great potential. He only needs you to be willing to go - so prayerfully consider serving in a greater capacity.

PUBLIC SYSTEMS

"Whenever you did one of these things to someone overlooked or ignored, that was me—you did it to me."

Jesus (Matthew 25:40 Message Bible)

Public Housing

Almost every city in our nation has a public housing program. Either many large compounds are spread across your town or federal funding is provided to local property owners that make available apartments or rental homes affordable to those living on or below the poverty level. These are excellent programs to provide reduced-cost housing for those who for reasons such as unemployment or a disability cannot afford standard housing costs. Depending on the size of your city, within this system are usually one or more staff members dedicated to helping residents access many social services. The staff arranges for things like tutoring or after school and summer programs for the children living there, medical education or information on community programs for adults. These can be things like literacy programs, how to write resumes and conduct online job searches, providing or delivering food boxes, and transportation for the elderly and shut-ins. Also they coordinate donations of Christmas gifts for the kids and backpacks filled with school supplies before school begins. They have budgets for some of these programs, but never enough to cover all the needs, and they require a great amount of community support. There might already be churches in your community reaching out with public housing programs. In my town there are churches that provide Vacation Bible School at some of the housing communities each summer for the kids. At certain times every year housing communities will have special events like a health or job fair and some participate in National Night Out (https://natw.org/) which is held every August on the first Tuesday. This is an annual community building campaign that promotes neighborhood camaraderie to make neighborhoods safer, more caring places to live. This event is similar to a block party with food and games and a fun time for all. It would be very easy for you to volunteer and set up a table to serve homemade cookies or cupcakes and get to know the residents living there.

What if you as an individual or a few friends in your church began to bless the public housing system in prayer? Pray for the people who live there. You might be surprised to learn that extended families have been there for two or three generations. God could use you to break this cycle of poverty off those caught in this generational disparity. Often public housing areas have higher rates of crime compared to other city neighborhoods. After you spend a period of time in prayer, then call to set up a meeting with the social services coordinator to ask is there any way you can volunteer to help. If you sense they are receptive to you mentioning you are from a faith based group or church fine. If not, simply say you are a concerned community member wanting to offer some volunteer hours. Be sure to listen to what their needs are and offer to help completely in line with what they are asking. If they need tutors for kids after school, then ask in what subjects and then volunteer as it is convenient for you and works with their schedule. If they have many children needing tutoring then find a few college or high school students or retired teachers you know that are willing to spend a couple of hours a week helping these kids. If you don't know of any available college students then contact student organizations through a local college or university to ask for help. Reach out to the faith based student organizations on campuses to enlist tutoring volunteers. Many of these student organizations are looking for projects to serve within the city - you have now done them the favor of bringing one to them. Aside from enlisting help from student organizations, many college students are required to perform several hours of community service each semester. Even many high school students are now required to have a certain number of volunteer hours each year.

As you volunteer or organize a group of volunteers, you may start out tutoring in math, science, or reading in order to meet the need. Within a few months, you might learn you have a student whose grandma is in the hospital, which is an opportunity for you to go and visit her, or a student without a winter coat. Right before your eyes you see the Holy Spirit move you from the city-reaching step of fellowship to meeting felt needs. You will discover felt needs you can meet without great cost or effort. While you do so you will be building relationships with people that likely would never have visited your church. Housing communities are often governed by a group called the "Resident Association." This is made up of individuals that live within this system and they normally meet monthly. Ask the social services staff member if you could start an "encouragement group" and offer to teach Bible studies on topics like managing your emotions, freedom from fear or parenting. You might facilitate a weekly group on any one of dozens of great books available on these subjects. Several of the ministers I've named in the Acknowledgement section have excellent materials both in printed form and in audio versions for your use. Once you make this request, the staff person will have to present the idea before the Resident Association for a vote. All they can do is to reject your idea. But what if they agree to it? Then you are on your way to offering spiritual encouragement to people you would never have met within your church.

For four years, I've assisted with a police officer mentoring program for children ages 8-14 in two of our public housing compounds.

One of the reasons for this program came from a survey conducted with the children living there. Many of them said their greatest goal in life was to have their own unit in the public housing community. We realized that they were often not exposed to opportunities that many children have to learn and explore the world around them. We started meeting once a month and taking the kids to local museums, the public library (no one in the group of twenty had ever been before), and to parks and many months we would just hang out together in a community center room at the location where they live. We have heard them tell about problems at home, being bullied at school, struggling with their grades, not having food, and have found any number of ways where we could encourage them. Another reason we have police officers involved is that we learned some of the children expressed negative attitudes towards police because they had family members who had been involved in the criminal justice system. In this setting they can see police officers as friends and mentors and not "the bad guys." Volunteers from a nearby Baptist church wanted to get involved with us in this outreach after we had been meeting about a year. One of these individuals started attending the monthly meetings and is now part of our leadership team. Over time, this individual really became familiar with some of the families. Since her church is close to this housing compound, whole families started attending the church weekly and even a few teens are now coming on their own. This church provides a lunch after services on Sunday, and housing families who attend stay to eat and fellowship. Church members are now mentoring teens and helping with them their school work.

Another service project involves my home church. Each year, church members adopt the kids in our program at Christmas and generously provide gifts for each child. The youth from my church pay for the food and serve at the Christmas party. My church also provides all the kids with backpacks filled with school supplies every year before school starts. Most recently a new open door with the housing communities is an expansion of their services to provide housing for unaccompanied youth. These are 18-24 year olds who have aged out of foster care yet have no home to live in or family to help care for them. In our housing community, the staffs try to arrange for each of these youth to have a mentoring team that helps encourage the young person to further their education, learn a job skill or gain employment. Regularly, there are not enough mentors for each young person to have this kind of support. I remember when I was between the ages of 18-24 - it's hard to think of going it alone completely at this age. Just a small commitment of time can make a big difference in the lives of these youth and their future. Ministry opportunities are endless within your public housing system, and it's very likely the doors are standing open to access the residents who are living there with the love of God.

Public Schools

Every city has a public education system for the children in kindergarten through high school. As with Public Housing, the school system often suffers from a shortage of resources. Begin by blessing in prayer all the public schools in your city. These are highly stressful environments for students and teachers alike. Pray for the safety of the school. The key to opening the door for city-reaching in the public schools is to find out if there is a teacher, coach, guidance counselor, or administrator in your church or neighborhood. These individuals will know best where and how you can volunteer or whom to contact to become involved. In my city there are several churches that over time have come along side our local public schools in many ways. One elementary school is located in an area of town where the student population is largely from lower income families. The principal of this school attends a large Methodist church in our downtown area. She told several in her church how children and families at her school did not have enough food to eat especially in the summer and on school breaks. A church member suggested organizing a meeting with all the churches in the district of this elementary school to discuss how they could start a food distribution program for the school. When they met, all six churches represented, were very open to the idea of participating. Together they came up with a system for making up food boxes to send home with families on a rotating basis. These churches are finding themselves meeting a felt need in the school and building relationships with some of the families.

A principal from another elementary school in town that has a high poverty level population attends a non-denominational church where she began telling church members about needs in her school. One need was that many of the kids had little or no involvement with their fathers. This church decided to start an annual "kick ball" league that has grown tremendously in three years. Each fall, registration opens for six weeks of kick ball and the children who sign up are divided into teams and play one night a week. The men of the church volunteer as coaches and other church members provide a meal for all the kids on game night. Each child receives a free T-shirt and trophies are awarded at the end of the kick ball season to every child who participated. Also the kids and their parents are told about a summer camp which the church offers and invites them to attend at no cost. Many of the kids then go from playing kick ball to attending a week of summer camp where they are presented with the gospel. The six weeks of kick ball helps build relationships between church members, the school kids, and their parents as well as providing "male figures" for children who otherwise would not have any in their lives. This church has been very successful with the kickball program, and doors have opened with opportunities to provide volunteers each summer who help the teachers set up their classrooms before students return to school and several of these volunteers serve as teachers assistants as needed during the school year.

One of the churches from a Christian Church denomination in my city which is located in a less impoverished area of town reached out to the principal of the elementary school to see how they could help. The principal responded of a need for tutoring and mentoring for many children in the school. Members of the church researched for existing programs they could use and found Kids Hope USA (http://www.kidshopeusa.org/home/) which they now have successfully implemented in the school for several years. Kids Hope USA develops these one-on-one relationships through the creation of church-school partnerships that pair church members with at-risk kids in supportive, mentoring relationships. Kids Hope USA mentors spend just one hour per week, reading, talking, playing and listening to a child at school. By helping the child feel loved and valued, they help that child to learn, grow and succeed. The outreach pastor of this church attended my Faith Based Leaders meeting at the police department to share with a group of pastors about the Kids Hope USA program. The program contains complete training materials for the mentors as well an orientation protocol for the school for a very small investment. Kids Hope USA started in 1995 with three churches partnering and since has grown to over 900 churches.

There are public school programs sponsored by several area churches in my city, and the director of outreach of the church with the kickball league began hosting a quarterly meeting for all the churches involved in ministering to the schools. This serves as a great time for volunteers to discuss obstacles they are experiencing in their various programs, share successes and pray together for the families and teachers who are represented by all of these schools. I facilitate a monthly crime prevention partner meeting of local agencies and a few staff members of the public school system frequently attend. These staff members also attend our bi-monthly Trauma Informed System of Care meeting. From school representation in these meetings, we have learned of specific needs. In our rural community, there are over 700 children attending public school who are considered "homeless." Some live on the street with their parent(s) but many others have no home address because they move from house to house frequently staying with relatives or acquaintances. When I learn information about needs within the schools from these meetings I share them with the Faith-Based Leaders group. These leaders share the needs within their congregations and spheres of influence to help assure that needs are met. Marketplace ministry growth has increased by following this approach.

Corrections Community

For four years I was involved very closely with the Corrections community under my grant program as we developed and ultimately implemented the first probation program of its kind within the state. Prior to the program, I knew very little about this population. Every year hundreds of thousands of people are released from state and federal prisons back into their communities. Depending on what state you live in, recidivism rates can range from 45-77% with these individuals returning to prison within one to three years. Over the past two decades the prison population in the United States has grown by 500%. Our country has the highest incarceration rates than any other country. Every state is now faced with keeping up expensive prison systems, but yet greater incarceration rates, has not equaled less crime. To improve public safety, communities must address prison overcrowding and reentry issues. It was surprising to learn how high the percentage of those incarcerated was due to drug-related crimes. These are crimes such as the possession of drugs, manufacturing drugs, selling drugs, or home invasions, theft and property crimes to pay for drugs. That is one reason why I was drawn to educating my community on the effects of adverse childhood experiences. Remember, a male who has experienced 6 of a possible 10 adverse childhood experiences is 4,600% more likely to be an IV drug user than someone with none. One of the co-creators of the ACEs survey stated that heroin was being used for relief of profound anguish dating back to childhood experiences and suggested that it might be the best coping mechanism many individuals can find. Since childhood abuse and neglect are so prevalent, it is no surprise there are a large number of communities that are facing a drug addiction epidemic.

Along with the complications surrounding drug addiction, the corrections community also finds it necessary to help offenders navigate the many barriers faced to successful reentry. Oftentimes these individuals have no transitional housing, no transportation, no valid driver's license and no one willing to even interview them for a job depending on the types of charges they have incurred. Every church and marketplace minister needs to pray for the corrections community within their city. One-stop shop reentry programs similar to the one we created are greatly needed in every town. In this program a returning citizen can receive addiction treatment, relapse prevention training, individual counseling, job and life skill training and community service opportunities. Many cities have a reentry collaborative that meets regularly to identify these barriers and how to remove them. Our collaborative meets once a month at the office of the Department of Corrections. Represented are people from employment services, faith-based groups, housing partners, addiction treatment programs and more. Locally, anyone is welcomed to attend these meetings. As you bless in prayer the corrections community, you can follow up by contacting your local office of probation and parole to see if such a group already exists in your town. By attending you can learn more specifically what are needs to reentry and in what ways you can help.

Employment needs are one of the greatest barriers to gaining successful reentry. As a group of business people involved in marketplace ministry or as members of a church, you need to consider starting a job training program. Individuals when released from prison are usually not ready to start taking classes at a technical or community college. However, they do need to gain employment because they have court costs and probation fines that must be met so they do not violate the conditions of their probation. Since individuals referred to our probation program would be attending at least twelve months before they can graduate our employment specialist researched the types of employment training available that could be offered as a part of our programming. She found a professional certification course in Customer Service and Sales that was available from the National Retail Federation (https://nrf.com/). For only a few hundred dollars from my grant I purchased the teacher materials and student workbooks for this forty hour course and then we offered two hours twice a week for ten weeks. The employment specialist further reduced the cost by having clients write their answers and solve problems in a three-ringed binder provided to them instead of in the student workbook so the workbooks could be reused. In this course, students learn basic work fundamentals and the nuts and bolts of retail business. The course includes, how to be customer focused, knowing your merchandise, and techniques used in selling. As we prepared to offer the course, we learned the closest exam center was in a town about 100 miles away. I partnered with an inner-city church that also had expressed an interest in teaching the course to some of its members, and together we qualified to become an exam center in our town. The pastor and I then took the training to be able to proctor the exam and for me, it has proven to be such a rewarding experience. It is a real joy to administer the exam to individuals involved in the criminal justice system who many have had years without an achievement as substantial as earning a national certification to raise their self-esteem. This course has been worth every penny! Once people started successfully earning their certification they have told me they were promoted from working the front line in a fast food restaurant to becoming a trainer or another received a pay raise that made them the highest paid server. One woman was hired by a retail chain that entrusted her with a key to the store and responsibilities for locking up after she told them she completed this training. Each of these individuals had a history of felony charges along with addictions, but now as they were gaining sobriety, this training raised their income levels to provide them with more livable wages.

The Customer Service and Sales Course was so successful, I began to research for other possible certifications we could offer within the probation program and discovered, "Guest Services Gold" (https://www.ahlei.org/Certifications/Line-Employees/). The program provides training for jobs in the hospitality industry in areas like breakfast attendant, guest room attendant, front desk representative, kitchen cook, maintenance employee and restaurant server. The teacher materials for this program are less that two hundred dollars, and the student books including the exam are very inexpensive as well. With these two educational opportunities we are able to offer short, professional certified trainings that prepare individuals for jobs that are readily available in the community. By taking these courses, many times they are promoted at work to increased responsibilities allowing them to earn higher wages. Along with teaching these skills you can offer training in resume writing, interviewing skills and how to do online job searches. Just as we did, you can begin to build a network with what we call "second chance" employers who are willing to interview candidates with prior criminal histories. Once or twice a year you could host a job fair with these employers. Your public library would likely be an accommodating host for the fair. Whether providing these trainings inside a probation program as we did, or within a public housing system or youth center, each of these certifications can be earned by attending classes only a few hours a night or on Saturday for three to six weeks depending on how long you stretch them out. Trust God that with His favor, you can find community sponsors to help offset the cost of the training materials and then pass along an affordable amount of the expense to the person enrolled in the training. By creating a job training center, you could not only impact the corrections community but also those living at the poverty level or for youth living in your town.

Every city could greatly benefit from this type of job training center if one does not exist. The only need is a classroom. The Guest Services Gold program doesn't require use of computers for testing. The Customer Service and Sales Course from the National Retail Federation require computers for testing but not for the training itself. In the future, we plan to propose offering courses in Keyboarding and Computer Skills as well as open a separate community job center aside from the one operating within the probation program. One community purchased a large truck capable of shredding documents and started a "shredding business." In our city, one of the credit unions offers financial recovery courses that they have taught to folks in the probation program. They were able to restore the credit of an individual who experienced identity theft while he was incarcerated. This credit union offers a program where a person who completes specific training goals, can apply for a micro loan of five hundred dollars which they can use to start a small business. Perhaps with these funds they could buy cleaning equipment or a lawn mower.

Employment needs are just one barrier facing citizens released from jail. Transitional housing is often scarce in communities, as is the case in my city. When someone who was incarcerated returns home, if they move in to live with family and friends, unfortunately these can be the very environments that contributed to their past crimes. There are state and federal transitional housing grants for the specific purpose of organizations obtaining "brick and mortar" and many of these grants welcome faith-based organizations to apply. Since these one-time grants are only for the purpose of purchasing or renovating an existing building to be used as transitional housing – there is no grant reporting required nor does the funding source interfere with your programming model if you are faith-based. Also in many states, it's likely your State Department of Corrections, will reimburse your organization up to 6-8 weeks rent for someone to live there after their release from prison.

Depending on what kind of housing is arranged, probationers will often need household items and even clothing. We created a clothing closet in our program to store both men and women's clothing that would be appropriate for wearing to job interviews. In our city, public transportation is limited. If someone gains employment that requires them to work until 8 p.m. at night, the transit system is not available. We were able to get donations of used bicycles which we loaned out to probationers in order that they have transportation to maintain their employment. A friend and member of our church has taught a Bible study in a prison near our community for several years. He and other volunteers from our church provide a free dinner and Bible study one evening a week as support for those released from prison. Our state corrections program has now launched a program inviting faith based organizations to provide mentoring for one offender for one year once they are released from jail. Many returning citizens need to make new friendships, and support systems as their old circle of friends and relatives may serve as opportunities to return to drugs and crime upon their reentry. In order to reduce prison overcrowding and help these individuals successfully rebuild their lives, this need must be shared by marketplace ministers and not the state and federal corrections systems alone. This is certainly a place where God can show Himself strong through you and you might end up in a place of influence in a prison system just like Joseph did or bringing reform to the reentry process like what I experienced!

Law Enforcement
Being a member of law enforcement has never been an easy job but having increased national tensions between police and community in recent years has only made it harder. Working inside a police department, I know how events of violence against officers affect the morale of officers and their families. To combat this, marketplace ministers and the faith community can come alongside and offer support to your local law enforcement. In the fall of 2015 after a deputy was gunned down in Houston, Texas while pumping gas into his patrol car, it seemed many in our community were contacting me asking for ways to show support to the officers in our department. I met with our Chief to discuss implementing a prayer support program I'd heard of through my involvement with Dr. Ed Silvoso's Transform Our World Ministry called "Adopt A Cop." (http://adopt. transformourworld.org/en/adopt-a-cop) The Chief told me that one of our chaplains and the president of the officers' wives organization had approached him recently with a similar idea to initiate a prayer support program for the officers. I met with these ladies to discuss implementing this in our department, and they responded very enthusiastically. The "Adopt A Cop" program works around a simple plan. Those who sign up commit to pray daily for an officer following the eight Prayer Points that are laid out in a brochure that you can download for free from Transform Our World. The Prayer Points include praying for the officer's physical safety, emotional strength, health at home, divine wisdom, financial provision, high morale, inner strength and spiritual strength. You can either sign up

on the Transform Our World website to pray for a cop, as a concerned citizen, or commit as we did, by offering the program to our whole department. In order to keep the information about our officers confidential, our chaplain assigned a number to each officer who enrolled in the program. When someone in the community would register as an adopter, our chaplain would send the volunteers the number of an officer for whom they can pray. The enthusiasm for this program spread like wildfire! In just a few months the program had over 1,400 adopters and numerous whole churches signed up to pray for our officers! As the local news reported on our Adopt A Cop program, two neighboring sheriff's departments in other towns contacted me about beginning a program in their cities. Regularly people deliver food to the department for the officers as well as a steady stream of cards of encouragement are received in the mail from adopters on a weekly basis.

Our police officers are involved in many ways with citizens outside of their regular law enforcement duties. We have started programs like "Coffee with a Cop" where officers come to a church, coffee shop, or business with no agenda or speeches planned, but only to get to know those who come. It's beneficial for police to have programming which provides an open forum for dialogue with citizens around current events on both a local and national level. I've worked with other city staff to organize events like "Party in the Park" where we have food trucks, provide inflatable's, enjoy live music, face painting, and officers along with their families enjoy an afternoon of fun in the park with residents. Begin by blessing your police department in prayer. Then contact your Chief, Sheriff or State Highway Patrol Captain's offices and ask if you or a small group of marketplace ministers can come to meet with them. Once this is scheduled, ask the law enforcement leaders how best you can show officer support. Suggest starting an "Adopt A Cop" prayer program. Most likely your leadership would be open to community member's show of support and even allow them to stop by and offer prayer. They know more than anyone how demanding and unpredictable a job in law enforcement can be. Ask if they have any community outreach programs similar to "Coffee with a Cop" and if not, offer to start one by setting up the first event. Be sure to listen to the leadership and set up programming within the parameters they define. For instance, our Chief did not want any personal information released to the public about the officers in the Adopt A Cop program. The chaplain adhered by creating the number system and giving adopters a random number assigned to each officer. In a large neighboring city one lady had a desire to show support for police officers so she organized about thirty women who bake homemade cookies for officers and deliver them on a regular basis. They call themselves the "Cookie Crusaders." These are only a few ways you can bless your police officers but it's a great place to start! I've read of another city where the police officers' union started a program, "Pray for Police" and anyone in the community can come by their office and pick up a wristband that simply says, "P4P"on the band and it serves as a reminder to pray daily.

Homeless Services
Cities in America have to answer the question of how to take care of a growing number of homeless individuals. The causes for homelessness vary from unemployment, poverty, and lack of affordable housing to people having significant histories of childhood abuse and trauma which can lead to mental illness, risky behaviors or a lifestyle of drug and alcohol addiction. Depending on the climate of your town your homeless population could be larger than others. Sadly, even when they are offered shelter, and various types of services, some individuals decline help and would rather remain out on the street. Increasingly in our city we see a larger number of young people between the ages 18-30 who are homeless. Generally, this population only wants to find a place to shower, do laundry, grab a meal and then are on their way again. It is a very dangerous lifestyle to say the least. There are many ways Christians can effectively minister to homeless people out in the marketplace. First of all, begin to

bless in prayer those who are homeless and all the agencies who serve them. This is not an easy ministry. Statistically, those being served have most likely suffered tremendous amounts of physical, sexual and emotional abuse in their lifetime so prayer for them is essential to their restoration. Secondly, contact several of the services in your city. It's not unusual to find that many are faith based organizations and likely would welcome volunteers, donations or help with outreach. There are meals to be cooked and served. In addition, some programs deliver meals or food boxes to those who cannot come to the location where they are serving. Also, there are day centers where homeless people can spend the day, do laundry, shower, and access case managers who will arrange for types of healthcare and other services they are in need of. These programs all need donations of sheets, towels, toiletries, diapers, and baby items.

In discussing "Corrections" I mentioned starting a job skill training center. Homeless individuals are another group of people who would greatly benefit from job skill training as well assistance with job placement. Networking within your city to locate area businesses that specialize in property maintenance to identify if any would be willing to provide a training program on operating machines like buffers is a great idea. Once an individual completed the training satisfactorily, the maintenance company might even consider hiring them. Our largest hospital system started a program whereby twice a year a job fair is held for the disadvantaged at the local public library. Several individuals have been hired by the hospital that now work in housekeeping or maintenance on a full-time basis and have healthcare benefits. Programs serving homeless individuals also welcome volunteers to help teach skills like resume writing or how to conduct online job searches. If your shelter services are faith-based, they may welcome you to attend a Bible Study they hold. Once you've attended awhile they may allow you to take a turn facilitating the group. The gospel IS the power of God so as you share God's Word have faith that His power is present and changing lives.

Every year cities are required to conduct a Point in Time count (PIT) of the homeless population. Usually this is done over a twenty-four hour period including through the night. Groups spread out to areas where it is known that homeless people are staying whether this is in a shelter, tent encampments or living in their cars. Each person counted is asked to complete a few questions on a survey. In our city the surveyors then give the person a bag of toiletry items as a thank you for participating. I have had the PIT count organizers attend the Faith-Based Leaders meeting at the police department to recruit volunteers and to recruit churches willing to donate and assemble hospitality bags. These are all small steps that contribute to making a big job much easier. The PIT count helps to determine the amount of federal or state funding a community receives towards providing certain types of homeless services. Therefore it must be done as accurately as possible. Often people are missed in this count because they are not living out on the street or in shelters but moving from house to house living with relatives, friends and acquaintances.

Every city has public services and systems similar to these that have been identified. There are other systems that have not been included at length like the Juvenile Justice System. Teenagers involved in the justice system could also benefit from a job training center similar to the one described above. They also need mentors for youth who do not have any stability or role models at home. Begin to look at all these systems in a new way. Recognize them as open doors for reaching the lost and befriending the unchurched. Even if you don't become involved serving with any of these organizations, you should commit to pray for them. A friend of mine, Dr. Lloyd Turner and his wife Joanne are co-founders of Pray For Newark, which launched the first citywide Adopt Your Street in Prayer initiative in 2007. This initiative enlists a person willing to bless in prayer daily a particular street. By the end of the first year, they had 33% of the streets in Newark adopted in prayer and the murder rate also dropped by 33%. For a city that had a long history of violence and despair this was one of the first indicators of change in the spiritual climate. Within two years Newark had 100% of the streets adopted for daily prayer. They experienced no murders for the first time in decades during a period of over 40 days. Also new businesses began to move in, the economy turned around, and the city began to return to life. Dr. Turner has written a book called "Street Adopters Handbook" (https://www.amazon.com/Street-Adopters-Handbook-spiritual-climate/dp/1500947490) where he shares the street adoption model which is now being replicated in over 300 cities around the world. Every city needs to launch this prayer initiative! If your town has not, begin by praying for the street where you live and work. God is looking for places to show Himself strong so let Him know your street is just that place. Remember we are not waiting on God to move within our city, He is waiting on us.

NON-PROFITS AND PRACTICAL SERVICE
OPPORTUNITIES

"Why, anyone by just giving you a cup of water in my name is on our side. Count on it that God will notice."

Jesus (Mark 9:41 Message Bible)

In this chapter, I discuss non-profits and other service agencies that are likely to exist in your town. Their names may vary but they provide the same services as what I describe. These agencies provide many open doors similar to the public systems where you can become involved influencing people in the marketplace.

Meals On Wheels

Most cities have a nutrition program such as Meals On Wheels that provide hot, healthy meals delivered to the homes of shut-ins or seniors who might not otherwise have a daily nutritious meal. In our community the program provides about 1,500 meals five days a week in an eight county area. The director told me that those who actually deliver the meals to the homes are sometimes the only person the resident sees all week. A few years ago she asked me if I knew of any youth groups who would be willing to make Valentine's Day cards that could be delivered with the meals. I thought this was a great idea so I shared it with several churches including my own. Since then, the youth group in my home church has made this a regular practice every February. This past year I reached out to the local at risk children and youth programs to see if the staff would want the kids they serve to make some cards. Every one of these agencies was delighted to participate! You could volunteer to deliver meals one day a week or even just one day a month. You could contact the director of the feeding program and ask about gathering cards from local churches or children's programs for Valentine's Day or other days of the year. These are such simple steps that can really make a difference. By doing so you will meet people in the marketplace you would have never met by just attending your church.

Community Gardens

Under my crime reduction grant, we committed to creating a Community Garden in one of the two high crime neighborhoods. Previously, I didn't know anything about Community Gardens but I have since learned they can bring blessing to a neighborhood in many ways. The first thing you need to do is identify a small lot that can be used indefinitely for the garden. You might consider an area located near public schools or public housing so you could start a gardening program for kids living there and then they can just walk to it. This is what we did. We had a housing developer donate a small lot attached to one of their rental properties that was too small to build another home on. We contacted the water department to turn on water. Then a plumber connected a spigot to the meter for a reasonable charge. I then contacted a gardening club at the university whose members jumped at the chance to get involved. We decided to plant fruit trees so there would not be an excessive amount of work if we found little community interest in the way of volunteers. Once we had a plan we talked to the neighbors on several blocks nearby as well as the staff at public housing about getting kids involved. Over time we have built a picnic shed and a pergola to grow vines and painted water barrels to catch rain for a sustainable water supply. Each year we invite the neighbors, college and high school students needing community service hours and kids from public housing to come to the garden for weeding, mulching paths, making signs, planting the seeds and harvesting the crops. We've made an event around it. Not only does working together provide a chance to build marketplace relationships, but the garden becomes a healthy food source that might not be otherwise affordable to those involved. You can use the garden to teach about nutrition which we have with our kids program. Working in the garden is popular with the probation program. Many individuals on house arrest are limited in the places they can go. They can volunteer and enjoy the sunshine outside while working in a garden. We have Probation Programs send a staff member to supervise groups that come and work for 2-4 hour blocks of time. One group even made salsa with the crop of peppers and tomatoes one year. There is no shortage of ways you can mix sharing the love of God within the context of a Community Garden.

Foster Care

Foster Care is an essential service in any city. Depending on the size of your state there could be thousands of children and teens who are living in foster care. Here I'd like to remind you of the information I shared in an earlier chapter, "Treat Your City with Kindness." Foster Care can be a lifesaving buffer for a child helping to mitigate the effects of their experienced childhood trauma. None of us pick to which family we will be born. Many children are born to parents who are addicted to drugs, living lifestyles of crime, or are incarcerated throughout much of a child's life. Children are placed into state custody whenever it is determined their home environment is not safe or stable. Due to a lack of foster parents willing to move from fostering the child to adoption, some children remain in foster care for several years moving from home to home. The years of a child's life can never be regained, and their experiences often shape who they become as adults. By foster parenting, you can be used in a powerful way to change the course of life for a child. One local foster agency called Youth Villages has a staff member who is a Christian and her role is foster parent recruitment. She is passionate about speaking to church groups, asking them to pray for the kids needing to be fostered and then explaining the program to potential foster parents. How much time would it take to just pray for one child who is lacking foster care? If you look up foster care services in your area, typically on their website they will show pictures of children waiting on permanent adoption. Start by blessing these children in prayer. Maybe the Lord will lead you to become involved as a foster parent or to reach out to the organization to see if there are other needs like clothing or tutoring for kids. When I think of all the demographics in my city, I can't help but remember what Jesus taught: when we visit or feed the sick or those in prison, help the orphans or give a cup of cold water to a child, it is the same as doing it unto Him. I think Jesus must have been able to look ahead and see the condition of our cities as He so accurately named the groups who needed His help the most. One day I stopped at an auto parts store to get new wiper blades for my car. When the salesman came out to put the new blades on he asked me what kind of work I did. He seemed surprised when I answered that I worked at the police department. He proceeded to ask me if I knew of any rehabilitative programs for treating drug addictions and went on to describe his difficult childhood. His reason for asking he said was that as a child he had been placed in foster care with a family that helped change his life immensely. Now he was graduating from college and looking forward to finding a job in his field. However, his older brother had not been placed in foster care and was addicted to drugs and could not hold a steady job. This short conversation is a perfect example of the difference foster care can make in the life of a child.

Safe Families
Safe Families (http://safe-families.org/) is a program that hosts vulnerable children through extended family-like support found from within the faith community. When crisis situations arise, parents or

caregivers may be unable to provide a safe environment for children, thereby putting them at risk for neglect or abuse. Many families do not live in a city where they have extended family members that can help, and child welfare systems are required by law to rescue only victims of the most blatant abuses so thousands of children annually are at risk. I have heard of preteen children left home alone for a week while a parent was hospitalized for emergency surgery. I was told of a third grader being left with a teenage cousin for a period while their parent had to travel to another state to take care of an older sibling who had been in a serious accident. These situations can be avoided with a Safe Families program. For two years I was blessed to serve on a team that launched this program in our city. From the moment I heard about Safe Families I could see it would serve to meet a great need in our community. It was easy to help promote this program among other service agencies as well as in the faith community. By providing short term, emergent care that keeps the child in contact with their parents during the separation, it is not as disruptive for the family as if the child is placed into state custody. What surprised me the most about Safe Families is their biggest source of referrals actually comes from the state. Safe Families provides all the training for the host families, and when a hosting occurs, they try to surround the hosts with resources (i.e. meals or transportation) to help make the hosting as smooth as possible. Though much shorter than traditional foster care, in a similar way, Safe Families provides children with the stability they need while their family is experiencing hardship. The program has been well received in my town and new host families from churches are signing up to help on a regular basis. Since this program is faith based, it provides a wide open opportunity to meet a felt need for the caregiver and their children and then build a relationship with them beyond the hosting. Several of the host families have done this, and some of the families hosted are now attending their churches. But where were these "fish" caught? Out in the marketplace!

Neighborhood Association Meetings

In the early 1970's a program called Neighborhood Watch (http://www.ncpc.org/topics/home-and-neighborhood-safety/neighborhood-watch) was launched and is now one of the oldest and most effective crime prevention programs in the country, bringing citizens together with law enforcement to deter crime and make communities safer. I was instrumental in starting two of these groups under my grant for the high crime neighborhoods we were working in at the time. These groups can serve to enhance public safety in your neighborhood while at the same time providing you a format to build relationships with your neighbors. Begin by blessing your neighborhood in prayer. Put on a pair of tennis shoes, walk around a few blocks nearby, and begin to pray. Then contact a few neighbors telling them you would like to have a meeting to talk about public safety. It only makes sense that neighbors learn to watch out for each other's property since you have more opportunities to keep an eye on things during your routine coming and going than do the police. Police work by a reactive approach. When a shift of officers comes on duty the officers are waiting on 911 calls to dispatch them to areas of town where someone is needing assistance. But with a neighborhood watch program you can identify troubled areas collectively then report your concerns to the police who might arrange a special detail to check out these concerns. This is proactive policing. Our neighborhood groups identify concerns and organize litter clean-ups. They also contact the City Codes Department, Public Works, Solid Waste or Fire Department asking them to come and address concerns with the group. One of our groups meets in a large high-rise building where many elderly residents live. This group decided for a while to have a pot luck supper on the meeting night. Other neighborhoods have joined in to host an event each year on National Night Out which I mentioned under Public Housing. One historic neighborhood located near our university has had for many years an annual "garage sale" at the beginning of each school year. This event has grown in recent year to attracting over 15,000 visitors. As you meet monthly or quarterly with your neighbors, you will build relationships that then open the doors for fellowshipping, meeting other felt needs beyond public safety and then opportunities for sharing the gospel.

Contact 2-1-1 or Contact Concern
Contact Concern or Contact 2-1-1 in most cities is a faith based organization that provides trained volunteers who are available to connect you by phone with free food programs, financial assistance for utilities or medical expenses, shelters, counseling services, support groups, battered women's shelters and addiction prevention or treatment. This service is completely confidential and available to approximately 95% of residents living in the United States. By calling 211 a volunteer can provide comfort to those struggling with loneliness, depression and major life changes by listening, encouraging and crisis intervention. 211 also offers reassurance by providing scheduled, daily calls to the elderly, homebound and anyone with limited contact with the outside world. The organization provides in-depth training for all volunteers. If you have a landline in your home, some organizations can set you up to place or receive 211 calls from your home without your personal number being recognized. What an opportunity this service provides for communities as well as an open door to those who want to touch lives out in the marketplace – sometimes without ever leaving your own home.

Domestic Violence Shelters or Family Justice Centers
Most cities are inundated with a serious domestic violence crisis. Often those living in abusive situations have experienced violence growing up in a home where they witnessed violence and now resort to violence in their own relationships. These can be the most dangerous calls for police officers to respond to and they create a confusing situation for children who are present. If a victim is being choked, beaten or harmed physically in any way and asks a child to call for help, when authorities arrive they likely will respond by arresting the perpetrator which then leaves the child feeling like it was their action

that resulted in their parent going to jail. Statistics show that on an average someone endures at least seven occurrences of physical violence before they will reach out to an advocacy program. Consider this scenario; an intimate partner is impaired by drugs or alcohol when an argument breaks out which then leads to a physical altercation. If the victim leaves the situation, they understand they might be losing their home, their car, their source of income, and may possibly be jeopardizing their relationship with their children. On top of that, the perpetrator has tried to convince them over time that their violent actions are the victim's fault. The domestic violence shelters that exist in your city must maintain secrecy about their locations to protect the safety of those who take refuge in them. In order to find out the needs of your shelters, check to see if they have executive offices you can contact to inquire of needs they might have. These programs provide training for volunteers and very often take donations of clothing (adult and child), sheets, towels, dishes, etc. These programs can be funded by grants, United Way or city and county allocations. However they are funded, the need is always greater than the funding. If you wanted to help with a fundraiser for the shelter, the director would likely be ecstatic!

A Family Justice Center (FJC) differs from a shelter though shelter services are among its many partners. This best practice model co-locates professionals representing most of the systems victims need to access in order to leave an ongoing violent situation. These services can include law enforcement, legal advice, prosecutorial help, child protective services and counseling. In this model, a victim only has to tell his or her story one time. The Family Justice Center staff helps them navigate through all the services they need for whatever type of action they desire to take. Sometimes victims will come to the FJC just to talk with someone or to create a "safety plan" should their situation dangerously escalate. The police chief enlisted my help writing a grant for an FJC. Recognizing the vast scale of these incidents across our state, the governor created a safety initiative to establish ten Family Justice Centers statewide. We were awarded funding to become one of these. After we received funding, it took two years to build a community collaborative of partners and secure a building for the center before we had our grand opening. This resource has become an effective tool in our efforts to reduce domestic and sexual violence. When we were setting up our center our site coordinator visited the Faith-Based Leaders meeting to educate churches on how they could become involved. Our FJC conducted a survey of services victims felt would be helpful to them in their journey out of this difficult situation, and their responses overwhelmingly indicated that they desired "spiritual" encouragement. It might be possible that the domestic shelter or Family Justice Center in your community would welcome a Bible Study or a chaplaincy program in which you could participate. If you are a church leader, invite the directors of these programs to address your church. It's probably no surprise to you that there are those in your congregation who could benefit from these services. If not for themselves, they might have a friend or relative who could.

Neighborhood Restoration Programs
From a crime reduction perspective having a healthy and well-kept physical environment in a neighborhood plays an important role. When properties get run down they attract crime. Crime operates under the cover of "darkness" and where there are overgrown, unkempt or darkly lit spaces this is an invitation for suspicious activities to occur. City government recognizes that older neighborhoods must not be forgotten or they can become a bastion for crime. This was the case in my town and the crime reduction grant we obtained was to target one of these older neighborhoods. In the nearly four years I worked to offer services in this neighborhood, I learned a lot about the people living there. Many lived in our town a long time and were now retired, elderly and even shut-in. They were former school teachers, principals, nurses, mechanics and business owners. When they bought their homes forty to fifty years earlier the neighborhood was flourishing with life and development. Over time city expansion

created other thriving new neighborhoods that reflected what theirs had been in years gone by. There are many marketplace ministry opportunities for these original neighborhoods! In our community there are faith based housing programs such as Habitat for Humanity and Appalachian Services Project (ASP).

Both of these work to identify housing or repair needs within their established criteria. In the neighborhood in which I was working to reduce crime, we partnered with ASP to bring services to a few families living there. The ASP Program Coordinator at the time told me they had thousands of summer volunteers coming in to do work but had not yet identified a sufficient number of projects. When I heard this, I did a mailer to the neighborhood announcing applications were being accepted for "free home repairs" to qualified applicants hoping this would generate new inquires. However in a neighborhood safety meeting I learned from residents that they thought this was a "scam" as surely no one was offering "free home repairs." Determined to see residents benefit from these services, I took a uniformed officer out with me a few hours several days going house to house explaining this was a legitimate offer and asking the resident to apply. I collected 21 applications during that week. Two properties qualified for extensive repairs which were completed that summer at no cost to the homeowner. One elderly family was trying to obtain custody of their grandchildren but because their home was in such ill repair, they had not been able to qualify. ASP arranged for their home to receive metal siding and new windows which completely changed how their home looked and decreased their electric bill by adding improved insulation. The ASP model is impressive. When they are working with the summer crews of faith based volunteers, each week they have a picnic with the volunteers and the home owner where the gospel is shared. One couple told me with tears in their eyes how much they enjoyed the teams of young people working on their home for several weeks in the summer and they looked forward to the weekly picnic and fellowship. Habitat for Humanity, another program, provides a plethora of services including home construction, neighborhood revitalization, financial responsibility classes and disaster relief.   There are a number of ways both organizations welcome involvement. They both enlist volunteers skilled and non-skilled in construction. They are both closely involved with the families they serve and often are a first-line provider to help those who could be at risk of homelessness. Marketplace ministers could volunteer not only their time but their resources to help families in need with housing repairs or new affordable homes.

I've learned the more time you spend in neighborhoods the more opportunities arise to fellowship and meet a felt need. I saw things like an elderly person who had a tree fall during a thunderstorm and did not have the finances to have it removed. I was able to contact a few churches who came to their rescue. Another time someone had old furniture that was damp and was full of mold but too heavy to move out of the house. So I arranged a group of volunteers who carried these items to the curb, and I scheduled with the Solid Waste Department to pick it up. By following the example of Jesus to be a servant, you will see the doors for ministry out in the marketplace open wide when you walk down the path of neighborhood restoration.

At Risk Youth Programs
All cities have some form of programming for at-risk youth and children. Likely these programs are focused on caring for children and youth afterschool and during the summer. In my city some of these are Boys & Girls Club, Big Brother and Big Sister, Coalition For Kids, and Girls, Inc. Without these effective programs, the school dropout and crime rates would escalate beyond what they currently are. These programs provide a safe place where kids are cared for, supervised and mentored. In an earlier chapter, "Treat Your City with Kindness" I talked about the prevalence of trauma and the impact that adverse childhood experiences can have in shaping the future of a child. It has been recognized for many years that at-risk youth programs provide the structure and nurturing that many children do

not get in the home. Now by understanding the science related to the brain development of children who are living in chronic stress, we know a child's brain is conditioned to operate out of survival mode instead of the areas of the brain designated to learning, thinking and regulating normal emotions. This then creates frustrations for a child trying to succeed at school which subsequently can lead to problem behaviors.   Many at-risk youth programs are faith based and even those that are not will welcome volunteers. These programs need tutors, coaches for sports programs, donations of food, and all types of equipment, buses and of course financial resources. Marketplace ministry is ripe here. Begin to bless in prayer your community at-risk youth programs. Then make yourself available to the leadership of one or more of these. Respond to assist in whatever way they might ask for your help. Normally in a program involving children, policies and insurance will mandate that volunteers have a background check and provide references. In our city one church organized a fall festival where they contacted police, fire and EMS to bring service vehicles out and they had vendors set up representing services families might benefit from. They had free food and games, and then their worship team played music, and a short message on God's love was shared. I participated as a part of the police department but I witnessed the group praying for several throughout the event. What is happening here? Eternal seeds are being planted into hearts. Those who volunteer to help coach sports programs cannot not only facilitate physical exercise but teach valuable lessons of good sportsmanship. You might be coaching a child that a grandparent brings because the child's parent is incarcerated or addicted to drugs.   In a few hours each week you provide nurturing that can dramatically alter the course of that child's life. Are you willing to pray about making an investment like this? You might find that doors will open to not only touch the life of the child but then bring the love of God to their families as well.

There are other open doors in your city besides these I've listed. You could help with programs related to the local public library or a "move in day" on college campuses, start a grandparent support program, do graffiti removal, sponsor a "prescription drug take-back" drop box, or do something as simple as adopting your street in prayer. We have also utilized events like Black History Month and Martin Luther King Day to organize a short march through town where we reflect on Dr. King's legacy and faith for the equality of all races. A wonderful African American pastor who is a friend of mine saw the video of the Adopt a Street prayer project in Newark, New Jersey that I showed during one of the Faith-Based Leaders meeting. He later contacted me with the idea of having a prayer walk and rally incorporated into an event for Black History Month. He had the idea to have city leaders walk through town and at each street corner a different pastor would offer up prayer. We have now done these three years in a row and they continue to grow. We have had two Mayors, a few City Commissioners, businessmen and women, our university president and other community leaders join in. It is an unforgettable sight to see a pastor praying over a city block while hundreds of marchers gather around from diverse groups. And even those who are unbelievers join in, showing respect for this holy moment.

I hope by now the Holy Spirit has convinced you that never again should you say, "We are waiting on God to move in your city." The truth of the matter is He is waiting on you to go. Ministry is waiting on you out in the marketplace through any one of these doors that I've identified as well as every day when you go to work. They are all standing wide open. People inside them are hurting, desperate and lost. Will you allow God to move in your city by daring to walk through them? Going doesn't require you to have the right education, talents or ability. God only needs your availability.

TO GOD BE ALL THE GLORY

*"If you are faithful in little things, you will
be faithful in large ones." Jesus*

(Luke 16:10 New Living Translation)

P salm 2 verse 8 says, "Ask of Me, and I will give you the nations as your inheritance, and the uttermost parts of the earth as your possession." For many years I have studied the Scriptures discovering who I am in Christ and what my inheritance contains as God's child and as a joint heir with Jesus. I've believed and continually exercise faith to possess redemption's purchased possessions of wisdom, peace, joy, divine health, material provision, favor and right standing with God. But in Psalms God is telling us to ask for another possession. That is - the nations. Throughout the Scriptures, the Holy Spirit interjects God's heart for whole cities and nations to be reached. We see Jesus' eluding to cities repenting in Matthew 11:21, "Woe to you, Chorazin! Woe to you, Bethsaida! For if the mighty works done in you had been done in Tyre and Sidon, they would long ago have repented in sackcloth and ashes [and their hearts would have been changed]."

There are many modern day examples of God transforming cities and nations through marketplace ministry. With all my heart, I believe God is raising up a generation who will dare to ask Him for their city and even their nation. We know from Jonah and the repentance of the city of Nineveh in a single day that this can occur. In the nearly five years I've worked at the police department, I have sensed Him calling me to ask for my city. I'm amazed how God's Blessing on my life and His favor have raised me up as a hub for coordinating acts of kindness and compassion all over the city to reduce crime and enhance public safety. When I hear of new challenges, I ask God how His kingdom can come to Earth and His will be done in that area as it is in heaven. Think about that. God desires that we make Earth like heaven. Do you think there is a drug epidemic in heaven or children are suffering from abuse and witnessing violence? Of course not! Though we have elected officials that govern our town, I've accepted there is a heavenly election on my life to participate in the spiritual harvesting of my city.

One qualification for service that stands out above all others is that you give all the glory to God. He is the One who loves our cities and offers to us a partnership as His hands and feet in reaching them. As things break forth in your city - some things small and some beyond your wildest imagination - recognize it is happening because God is with you. The harvest is out in the marketplace. As you go, you will begin to see how much God loves those you choose to serve. I have cried as I heard their stories. I have prayed for solutions to rescue them. All along I knew that it was because of God inside me that I felt such compassion. Establishing the kingdom of God in the earth is a "family business." My heart is touched when I see the homeless, addicted, unemployed or hurting only because I have God's nature inside me, and His heart is moved by these same things. Many times in the gospels, we read where Jesus was moved with compassion and healed the sick, touched the children or fed the five thousand. What would it look like in the marketplace in our day for Jesus to show compassion? He is the same yesterday, today and forever so His compassion has never been withdrawn. Maybe He wants to work through you to bring reform to your state corrections program by providing new models of treatment. Only God can take the credit for my having any part in that. Remember I told you that when I first read my crime reduction grant and saw one outcome was to reduce recidivism that I had to look up the word in the dictionary to learn its meaning? Now with amazement I see in the news the Commissioner of our State Corrections Department discussing the state-wide replication of a program that was started under my oversight. Almost daily I'm contacted by a professional wanting to know who they can contact to learn more about the impact of adverse childhood experiences. In a little over one year, we've helped over 1,400 professionals to be trained and now at least three departments in our state university are incorporating this education into their course work. I've seen neighborhoods cleaned up, graffiti removed and street lights added. I'm frequently called upon by my department to take on new challenges in the community. Local leaders in business, education or humanitarian services seek out my assistance and counsel for their programs. No one is more aware than I am that to God alone goes all the glory! To those who are faithful in little, God will entrust much.

As you begin to bless your city in prayer and walk through the welcoming doors outlined in this road map be faithful with whatever God provides for you to do. It might start out a game of kickball with a little child who has no contact with his father and grow into a city wide program that touches hundreds of kids and their families. Expect God's grace to superabound in the marketplace. As it does, purpose in your heart to be like the one leper among the ten whom Jesus healed that returned to offer thanks. God has said that He desires to fill the whole earth with the knowledge of His presence. Without Him, you can do nothing, but you will represent Him in His power as you go. Now... are you ready to go? Your city is waiting on you.

ACKNOWLEDGMENTS

The Apostle Paul prayed for the early Christians in Ephesians 3:19, "That you may really come to know (practically, through experience for yourselves) the love of Christ, which far surpasses mere knowledge (without experience); that you may be filled (through all your being) unto the fullness of God (may have the richest measure of the Divine Presence, and become a body wholly filled and flooded with God Himself)!" Paul had been given by the Holy Spirit the revelation of the fullness of redemption that came through the work of the cross and resurrection of Jesus Christ. He understood redemption was so generous on God's part that prayer was needed for Christians to be able to comprehend and experience this amazing love.

I've always loved reading testimonies by people who have experienced God's love in their lives. It's one thing to know God loves you, and see others experience it, but then its life changing when you get to experience His love for yourself. It's like hearing someone describe eating a delicious meal, but how much better when you actually get to taste it for yourself? I worked many years in a university and often courses are taught by utilizing a lecture and a lab. In the lecture you hear knowledge about the subject but in the lab you experience the knowledge. This book is an account of things that I have learned all while experiencing God's love for me.

The most important acknowledgment as I share my journey is to express my gratitude to God for His love and unwavering faithfulness to me. Over the four decades since becoming a Christian, He has revealed Himself to me predominately by His written Word. Within His promises He has shown me how very much He really does loves me. In my brokenness, He found me and put me back together. He went on to reveal that He has faith in me and desires to accomplish great things through His Divine destiny for my life. I've come to learn that He is also good. He is not just good, but He is the Source of ALL goodness. His mercy and goodness follow me every day of my life (Psalm 23:6). I'm never meant to live one day without His goodness! It is in coming to know how good God is towards me that an immense desire has grown in my heart to share this knowledge with others. Ephesians 2:10 says, "For we are God's [own] handiwork (His workmanship), recreated in Christ Jesus, [born anew] that we may do those good works which God predestined (planned beforehand) for us [taking paths which He prepared ahead of time], that we should walk in them [living the good life which He prearranged and made ready for us to live]." Regardless of our past, our shortcomings or failures, God declares we are His handiwork and His workmanship. For those who are His handiwork, He says, He has already prepared paths for us and these paths are ones that lead us to living a good life.

I enjoy traveling. In the computer age in which we live, you can act as your own travel agent. You can secure online hotel reservations, book a flight, rent a car and just about anything you need to do in regard to your trip. Once all your arrangements are confirmed you create a travel itinerary. How comforting is it to know that the Author of your life has already planned your life "itinerary?" Not only has He planned it but He said it's a path to live a good life! Once I realized this, it changed my whole approach to walking in God's will for my life. Since He has already created this itinerary, I don't have to ask Him to create a plan, but rather I thank Him daily for His plan and that my steps are guided down the paths He already chose for me. It's by traveling on that path that I have come to discover the truths that I'm sharing in this book. Things I've experienced since beginning to work for the police department in 2012 are far from anything I could have ever imagined He had in His plan for me. On this path, I discovered a road map which I'm laying out in this book, to help you recognize and walk through new doors in your city where you can impact the lives of thousands who are hurting and unchurched.

I also want to acknowledge others along God's paths that have helped me. Without their influence, I might not have stayed on His itinerary or ever really understood it. First of all I'd like to acknowledge my deep appreciation for Kenneth and Oretha Hagin, or "Mom and Dad Hagin" as they were known to us at Rhema Bible Training Center. When I graduated from high school in 1976, MY plan was to attend secular college, obtain a teaching degree and possibly have a career as a teacher and coach girls' athletics of some kind as I had always been athletic myself. In the summer before I was to leave for college, God began impressing on my heart that He had His hand on my life to be used in ministry. At 19 years old I can't say that I really understood what that meant but I knew I wanted to follow Him more than anything. So instead of enrolling in a secular college, I had heard at church about this new Bible College in Tulsa, Oklahoma. I ended up traveling 920 miles away from home to attend Rhema Bible Training Center. I was there for two years and graduated in 1979 and feel so blessed that Dad Hagin was there daily to teach a class, lead devotions or in some way interact with us on campus. I'm thankful that he obeyed when God put in his heart to start a Bible training center. Now thousands of lives like mine have had the privilege to be impacted by his ministry and gain a revelation of the Spirit-filled life and how to walk by faith, all by looking to the pages of God's Word. Today Rhema graduates cover the earth teaching the Word of God and I am grateful to be one of them.

I also want to acknowledge my appreciation for Joyce Meyer, Kenneth and Gloria Copeland, Jerry Savelle, George and Teri Pearsons, Bill Johnson, Andy Mason, Andrew Wommack, Bill Winston, Ed Silvoso,

Lloyd Turner and Creflo Dollar. These are only a few from many, whose ministries have been an influence on my spiritual growth over the last forty years. It has also been these who God used to impart the specific truths into my heart that are the core of this story unfolding. I've only met five of these individuals in person but over the years I have attended many of their conferences, read bundles of their books and listened to countless hours of their Bible teachings. Listening to them in the early years was by cassette tapes, and then CD's came along and more recently by podcasts, streaming live or on-demand or by YouTube. Not only have their ministries impacted my life but their examples of faith have as well. I've learned through these individuals how to grow spiritually and be committed to living a life of excellence. I've learned from them truths on how to walk in love, practice forgiveness, renew my mind, manage my emotions, live under grace not the law, be faithful in the small things, take the limits off, expect God's favor, practice principles of sowing and reaping, how to walk in the miraculous, implement prayer evangelism, expect city transformation, how to practice diligence, patience and per-sistence and to never, ever quit. I'm publicly thanking them for their impact upon my life. I hope my story might encourage each of them to know that their ministries touch the lives of many who then impact their families, churches, and cities in ways they may not even know about and often won't know of until heaven.

Gratefully I also acknowledge my pastors, Dr. Barry and Rev. Ann Burns. They have been the pastors of Cornerstone Church, which has been my home church since 1975. They were co-founders of the church and when I left to attend Rhema Bible Training Center in 1977, I was the only student I knew of that came from a Sprit-filled church that taught about faith in God's Word. For over 40 years, they have labored faithfully in ministry with the grace and determination that few possess. For over two decades they employed me as a staff member where they gave me numerous opportunities to grow and experience ministry on so many levels. They showed me grace when I made mistakes and stretched me beyond my comfort level in many ways. Not only as Pastors but as two of my dear friends, their example of being "the real deal" in the pulpit and out of it has influenced my life in countless ways. Ever since entry into marketplace ministry in 2004, they continue to offer their constant support, friendship and encouragement for which I will always be grateful.

I want to acknowledge the love and support of my sons David and Christopher who will never know the joy they have brought to me as their mother. Both of them have such tender hearts for God and the men they have become as they embark on making families of their own makes me continually grateful for them. In some of the hardest places in my life, it was their love and encouragement that helped me to see that God had not forgotten me. I am certain God has great things in store for both of their futures. I'm thankful also for their families as we continue to grow in size. Each one is such a big part of making our lives abundantly blessed.

Lastly is one who without, this book would not exist. My husband Jonathan of 33 years has recognized God's call on my life from our first date. We met at Cornerstone Church in 1983. The first time he asked me out I agreed to go but proceeded throughout that date to explain to him I was going to marry a pastor one day. For some rea-son he continued asking me out and I would go, yet all the while hold-ing to my story that I was going to marry a pastor one day. Finally after a few months of spending time together, he said to me, "Can you just give our relationship a chance?" "After all," he added, "Jesus was a carpenter!" – which as you might guess, is his trade. Within a few months after that, we became engaged and the rest is history. The thing I love about Jonathan the most is his steadiness and sense of stability. In the early years of our marriage, even though I was a born again, Spirit-filled Christian, I experienced times where I was uncontrollably tormented in my mind and emotions. Jonathan was so constant in loving me even though he never knew from one day to the next whether I'd be up or down. To me he has exemplified God's unchanging love for me.

It has been Jonathan who has witnessed my sense of wonder at the extraordinary things I began to experience one after the other since I came to work at the police department. He knew more than anyone that what was happening was beyond my own capabilities. Many times he has said to me, "You need to write a book." However, I never took his suggestion seriously at all until last summer when I began praying about ways God could use my story to encourage other Christians. I knew that others could experience what I have, with God's life inside them by flourishing in the hard places. God could raise them to places of influence in their community or company where they recognize wide open doors for reaching the hurting. During this season of prayer, Jonathan and I were vacationing at the beach and I was praying one day and reading Deuteronomy 28. Verse one says, "If you will listen diligently to the voice of the Lord your God, being watchful to do all His commandments which I command you this day, the Lord your God will set you high above all the nations of the earth." After reading that verse I simply said, "Lord is there anything I'm not listening to You about?" and immediately He brought to mind, Jonathan's encouragement to write a book. Somehow this time the idea was different. As I thought about writing a book, I recognized it now as an assignment from the Lord which I should no longer set aside. Now, I'm humbled to be sharing with you my story.

Made in the USA
Columbia, SC
05 November 2020